■ Freud and Faith ■

■ Freud and Faith ■

LIVING IN THE TENSION

KIRK A. BINGAMAN

State University of New York Press

Published by
State University of New York Press, Albany

© 2003 State University of New York

For information, address the State University of New York Press,
90 State Street, Suite 700, Albany, NY 12207

Production by Judith Block
Marketing by Michael Campochiaro

Library of Congress Cataloging-in-Publication Data

Bingaman, Kirk A.
    Freud and faith : living in the tension / Kirk A. Bingaman.
        p. cm.
    Includes bibliographical references and index.
    ISBN 0-7914-5653-6 (alk. paper) — ISBN 0-7914-5654-4 (pbk. : alk. paper)
    1. Psychoanalysis and religion.   2. Freud, Sigmund, 1856–1939—Religion.
    I. Title.

BF175.4.R44 B56 2003
261.5'15—dc21   2002067032

10 9 8 7 6 5 4 3 2 1

Contents

Acknowledgments

I thank colleagues and friends who have taken the time to read and provide me with constructive feedback on this project. Lewis Rambo has provided guidance and direction, from the project's beginning to its end. Rosemary Chinnici, James Jarrett, and Ted Stein have read and commented on earlier drafts of the manuscript.

The Lloyd Center Pastoral Counseling Service in San Anselmo has been a source of support and enouragement. I am indebted to Sandra Brown who has read several drafts of the manuscript, and has given me feedback on methodology and editing. Ruth Ann Clark has directed my clinical training, providing me with the opportunity to apply theory and theology to practice.

I am grateful to colleagues and friends and students at the San Francisco Theological Seminary in San Anselmo and at the Graduate Theological Union (GTU) in Berkeley. As an instructor in the course on Religious Conversion, where the project had its inception, I was working as a recipient of the Henry Mayo Newhall Fellowship Award. The religion and psychology department of the GTU was where this project got off the ground and began taking its distinct shape.

I thank Judith Block, senior production editor, and Nancy Ellegate, senior acquisitions editor at State Univeristy of New York Press, for their guidance, from the beginning to the end of the formal publication process. I thank Oxford University Press for permission to include revised portions of the forthcoming article by Kirk A. Bingaman, "Teaching Freud in the Seminary," in *Teaching Freud in Religious Studies*, ed. Diane Jonte-Pace in the introduction and in chapter 5 of this volume. And, I thank Kluwer Academic/Human Sciences Press, for permission to reprint the revised, "Teach Your Students Well: The Seminary and a Hermeneutics of Suspicion," *Pastoral Psychology* 48, no. 2 (1999): 99–105.

I thank Diane Jonte-Pace for previous collaborative projects, and more immediately, for her help with this particular project. I am grateful for her generous and thoughtful foreword to the book.

Finally, I am most grateful for the support and encouragement I have received from my mother, father, and brother, Brad. And, to my wife, Sam, and daughter, Anne, thank you for patiently and generously tolerating my absences and busyness.

Foreword

In 1939 the poet W. H. Auden wrote in memory of Sigmund Freud

> He wasn't clever at all: he merely told
> the unhappy Present to recite the Past
> like a poetry lesson . . .
> if often he was wrong and, at times, absurd,
> to us he is no more a person
> now but a whole climate of opinion
> under whom we conduct our different lives.

> W. H. Auden, *Collected Shorter Poems 1927–1957*

Deeply aware of the "climate of opinion," the moments of absurdity, and the "poetry lessons" that Freud embodies today, Kirk Bingaman asks us, in *Freud and Faith*, to take Freud seriously as a guide on a journey toward deeper faith. His goal is nothing short of metanoia in the lives of believers: he urges a rejection of the fear of Freud and a transcendence of simple faith.

Bingaman reiterates the central question asked by Paul Ricoeur in *Freud and Philosophy*: Can psychoanalysis purify the faith of religious believers? Ricoeur argued more than three decades ago that religious believers are obligated to "converse" with Freud, to expose religious faith to a Freudian hermeneutics of suspicion. Bingaman knows how difficult this conversation can be, yet he also knows how necessary it has become. He extends Ricoeur's question to the psychical lives of believers and to the specific projects of theological and religious educators, parish ministers, pastoral counselors, psychotherapists, and spiritual directors.

Acknowledging that for the believer Freud evokes hostile resistance, Kierkegaardian fear and trembling, or, at best, defensive indifference, Bingaman pursues a double project. First, he urges that believers respond to Freud with both yes-and-no. He recommends a resounding "no" to the enlightenment Freud for whom religion is always immature and neurotic; a "no" to the Freud for whom God is nothing but a projection; a "no" to the Freud for whom God is excluded from ultimate reality. He would say "yes," however, to the Freud who understands and critiques the dynamics of immature faith; "yes" to the Freud who articulates the problematic attraction of the God of consolation and constraint; "yes" to the Freud who finds meaning in imagination and psychical reality. His yes-and-no holds Freud in dialectical tension.

Bingaman's second goal is to coax the naive believer out of the simplistic and rigid dynamics of belief toward a more flexible, complex faith through the encounter with Freud. The God of moral condemnation, tolerated in exchange for a secure sense of eternal protection, he argues, must be seen as a mere projection of the oedipal father of childhood. This God must be abandoned. The loss of this oedipal God will involve great pain and will necessitate deep mourning, but, Bingaman promises, the loss will eventually result in a sense of enlarged faith through an encounter with the divine beyond oedipal projections. Bingaman sketches a modern-day resurrection: a death and renewal of faith.

A yes-and-no to Freud is thus closely interwoven with a loss and renewal of faith. Bingaman acknowledges that believers will face an arduous journey, full of obstacles, pain, and difficulty. Bingaman's companions on this journey with Ricoeur from simple to complex faith—and from simple dismissal of Freud to a nuanced position of mixed acceptance and rejection—are Ana-Maria Rizzuto and Judith Van Herik. Rizzuto's revisionist psychoanalysis in *The Birth of the Living God* reveals that a variety of parental roles—oedipal fathers, preoedipal mothers, and others as well—underlie the developmental history of God images. For Rizzuto some of these God images are benign and adaptive. And, she argues, the realm of psychical reality is not necessarily in conflict with truth. Rizzuto accompanies Bingaman into the territories of complex faith and mature response to Freud.

Van Herik's companionship on this journey is more complex. In *Freud on Femininity and Faith* she demonstrates the necessity of coming to terms with Freud if we wish to understand ourselves and our world. But she models an analytic stance to Freud and faith that is different from Bingaman's yes-and-no response. She neither mounts a critique of Freud nor claims that he is correct. Rather, she exposes the deeply intertwined structures of Freud's asymmetrical theories of gender and religion. Within the logic of psychoanalytic theory, the feminine is analogous to religious faith: both involve submission to

an oedipal father, and both are devalued. Van Herik's analysis of Freud's devaluation of the psyche of the believer and of the psychical world of women,
Bingaman suggests, may offer to the resistant believer a more palatable introduction to Freud's theory of religion than the dangerously ambivalent yes-and-
no encountered in Ricoeur and Rizzuto. Van Herik's interest is in the structural
dynamics of Freud's theory, rather than in using Freud to promote faith. This,
it might be said, makes Van Herik a companion on the journey toward deep-
ening the *conversation* with Freud that Bingaman adapts from Ricoeur, but not
in the *conversion* that is Bingaman's ultimate goal. Like Virgil escorting Dante
through the first levels of the *Divine Comedy*, Van Herik escorts Bingaman
through the first stages of his journey.

Bingaman is not the first to challenge contemporary believers to take
seriously Ricoeur's question, nor is he the first to promote a move from rigid
belief to open faith. Few, however, have been able to give the yes-and-no
response to Freud that Bingaman so carefully constructs in this religious
context. The double metanoia that Bingaman frames is innovative and original. In our contemporary "climate of opinion," paradoxically, "we all speak
Freud," as Peter Gay has said, and Freud is under continuous attack. In this
context Bingaman asks us to study *Freud and Faith*, charting an arduous but
important journey for religious believers, educators, and practitioners.

Diane Jonte-Pace
Santa Clara University

Introduction

The test of a first-rate intelligence is the ability to hold two opposed ideas in the mind at the same time, and still retain the ability to function.

F. Scott Fitzgerald, *The Crack-Up*

■ BACKGROUND ■

My interest in Sigmund Freud, to the extent of devoting an entire book to him and his theory, began taking shape several years ago in the context of the praxis of the seminary classroom. I was giving a lecture on the classical psychology theorists and their interpretations of religion to the Religious Conversion class at the Graduate Theological Union (GTU) in Berkeley. While addressing Freudian theory, I noted that according to Freud we human beings are born into an unfriendly world where at every turn the forces of nature—natural disasters, disease and illness, death, and so forth—threaten to destroy our lives. And while it is true that civilization, in response to these powerful forces, provides us with a certain measure of protection, this protection comes at a steep price: protection in exchange for instinctual renunciation, the suppression of our deepest biological longings and desires. I explained to the class that Freud believed that religion arose out of this less-than-satisfying state of affairs, a response to our fear of the forces of nature and to our frustration in the face of an oppressive human civilization. Religion, then, and especially the promise of a rewarding afterlife, is our compensation for patiently and resolutely enduring our present travails and sufferings.

Freud, I went on to tell the class, theorized that as children we look to our parents, especially our father, when we feel helpless and threatened and in need of protection. Later, as adults, we discover that adulthood does *not* signal the end of feeling helpless, as we had innocently and naively expected. Therefore, in response to this prolonged feeling of helplessness, we begin to *project* onto the screen of the universe a supreme being who has the features of an earthly father, a being powerful enough to relieve our existential anxiety. Religion, Freud concluded, is the projection of our own human subjectivity onto a Rorschach-like cosmic figure, who supposedly has the capacity to satisfy our longing for protection and consolation in the face of life's hardships and disappointments. We create, in response to the fear and insecurity associated with feelings of helplessness, a God in our very own human image, a God who will seemingly fulfill our wish for eternal security.

It was Freud who would not let us forget that even though we, as adults, feel somewhat in control of our lives, we still and always will find ourselves surrounded by potentially hostile and threatening forces. In an attempt to cope with these forces, we intuitively link the ambivalent—protective *and* threatening—power of the unconsciously remembered father of childhood with a similar ambivalent power that we find in nature. We then personify the powerful forces of nature as God, and try through our religious devotion and piety to relate favorably to this God, just as we tried as children to relate favorably to our earthly father. As the powerful and inherently subjective image of the father of childhood gets projected onto the forces of nature, it acquires such titles as the familiar, "God the Father Almighty," which we find in the Apostles' Creed of the Christian faith.

Freud, of course, was not the first to put forward the theory that religious faith is the projection of our own subjectivity, stemming from the longing for consolation and protection in the face of life's disappointments and frustrations. Ludwig Feuerbach, in his book, *The Essence of Christianity*, a tour de force that "burst like a bombshell on the German intellectual scene in the early 1840s," had already concluded that "the idea of God is the unconscious projection of the essential human predicates, which is then regarded as a single, separate, heavenly being."[1] The idea of religion as projection, however, is even older than Feuerbach and the nineteenth century. In fact, this very theme can be detected as early as the sixth century B.C.E., in the writings of the pre-Socratic philosopher, Xenophenes. Xenophenes had astutely observed that human beings, to some extent, create gods in their own image, even down to such things as racial differences: "Ethiopians make their gods flat-nosed and black, the Thracians let theirs have blue eyes and red hair."[2] Thus, even though we often associate the theory of religion as projection with Freud, the fact is that he was hardly articulating an original idea. Nevertheless, Freud's work on the issue of religion as projection has been uniquely and extraordinarily influential in the Western world, largely because of his prominence as the founder and shaper of psychoanalysis and his distinctive articulation of the psychological dynamics at work in religious faith.

For this reason—Freud's extraordinary influence in the West and the fact that those of us living in the West have internalized so much of his theory—the philosopher and theologian, Paul Ricoeur, has argued that the religious believer is obligated to "converse" with Freud, and to expose his or her religious faith to a Freudian "hermeneutics of suspicion." Ricoeur offers no guarantees, except that the believer will not and cannot, following the encounter, be the same person with the same faith. In other words, an encounter with Freud presupposes an element of risk. Yet, because of Freud's extraordinarily influential critique of, and challenge to, religion, the greater risk for the religious believer "lies in avoiding the encounter altogether."[3]

Moreover, what religious believers will have to concede, after they have encountered Freud objectively with a reasonable degree of critical distance from their presuppositional biases, is that he not only deserves a "no" but also a "yes"; Freud did not get *everything* right about religious faith, but he still managed to get *some* things right. The religious believer, argues Ricoeur, is therefore obligated to hold religious faith and Freudian theory in dialectical tension, rather than opting to embrace the totality of one while rejecting the totality of the other. I concluded my presentation to the class by indicating that if we take Ricoeur's words to heart, this will then have major implications not only for our own personal religious faith but also for theological education, for the practice of pastoral care and counseling and for spiritual direction. Said another way, if we take Ricoeur as our guide, we will begin making Freud and his theory more of an integral part of theological education and spiritual formation.

Up to this point, the lecture had gone smoothly, with few interruptions—hardly any questions or comments from members of the class. My sense was, and is, that as long as we discussed Freud in a general and detached, that is, safe, sort of way students could acknowledge without too much difficulty that the field of psychology and even that of pastoral care and counseling owes something of a debt to Freud. But to up the ante, by bringing Ricoeur and his philosophy of "total engagement" with Freud into the discussion, was more than some of these students could tolerate. I remember one student, in particular, who raised his hand and very angrily proceeded to inform the class that we, in the seminary, have no business devoting so much of our time to an atheist like Freud, "someone who's nothing but a false prophet." The implication, it seems, was that because

Freud came down on the "wrong side" of the issue, religious believers are not obligated to take him and his theory of religion seriously.

For the past few years, from that lecture in the seminary classroom to the present, I have been gripped by an interest that is twofold: (1) Freud's theory that religious faith is psychological projection, and (2) the responses that Freud and his theory of religion evoke in the religious believer. In a sense, I have been "testing" Ricoeur's hypothesis—the religious believer is obligated to hold Freud and religious faith in dialectical tension—in the context of theological education, and I have witnessed a variety of emotional responses: anger or distancing, on the part of students who steadfastly refuse to take a class or join a discussion on Freud, and apparent mass indifference on the part of a large percentage of the student body, whose members from the beginning keep Freud at arm's length presumably because he has nothing constructive to offer the believer. Though the emotions and responses differ, there is at least one unifying feature: an aversion to Freud. Students in the field of theological education often do not take the time to engage and/or reengage Freud and his theory of religion, let alone acknowledge, with Ricoeur, that Freud did manage to get some things right about the psychological and cultural dynamics of religious faith. Some students, it is true, do take the time to engage Freudian theory, but they are a decided minority.

It appears, then, that what we often encounter in communities of religious faith is an attitude toward Freud that can be summed up in one word: *suspicion*. Believers, as I discovered firsthand, will point out that since Freud reduced religion to little more than the projection of our own subjectivity onto a perceived cosmic provider and sustainer of the universe, he has nothing to teach us about religious faith. The *Dictionary of Pastoral Care and Counseling* lends additional support to this thesis: "The full meaning of [recent] developments within psychoanalysis has yet to be adequately explored by Christian theology," primarily because of Christianity's "distaste for Freudian theory."[4]

This "distaste for Freudian theory," I would argue, is manifested in the context of theological education, clinical practice, and ministry anytime individuals, when confronted with Freud's challenge to religious faith, move into an "either-or" position vis-à-vis Freud rather than attempting to live within the dialectical tension between faith and psychoanalysis. The "data" from the seminary classroom, as well as the "data" from the pages of the *Dictionary of Pastoral Care and Counseling*, would thus appear to support the earlier research of William W. Meissner. Meissner, in his book, *Psychoanalysis and Religious Experience*, had found that "despite many years of effort by

to creatively live with the tension

pastoral counselors of all religious faiths, an attitude persists among the clergy that is antithetical to any psychiatric, psychological, or psychoanalytic intervention. The stalking-horse of Freud's secular and antireligious pronouncements and the myth of libidinal license still haunt the view of many."[5]

Now it must be remembered that religious believers are presently situated in a particularly complicated postmodern world that seems to be getting more confusing with each passing day. And, in an attempt to make this world more manageable and understandable, believers sometimes reduce their faith to the simplest possible terms, or to the lowest common denominator. The world already has more than enough puzzling conundrums, so why add more? Moreover, doesn't religion exist to offer the human individual a measure of solace and comfort in the midst of the chaos of daily living, a measure of the peace that transcends human understanding? Besides, religion and theology, in and of themselves, have more than enough complexities, as any seminarian can tell you, without adding someone like Freud and his theory to the mix. And yet, religious faith *cannot* be reduced to simple terms, for it is by nature a complex phenomenon. Therefore, it is essential to examine the phenomenon of religious faith and Freud's theory of faith as psychological projection from the vantage point of different fields and disciplines.

The representatives who I will be selecting from these different fields and disciplines all share one thing in common: the conviction that it is a serious mistake for the religious believer to respond to Freud dismissively, even before encountering his writings. Ricoeur, one of the theorists, acknowledges that in engaging Freud and his theory of religion, the believer does in fact risk becoming a different person with a different faith, and *will* become a different person with a different faith. It should therefore come as no surprise if believers are somewhat resistant to Ricoeur's suggestion, since he seems to be saying that an encounter with Freud presupposes the risk of change to self and to one's personal faith. This book, however, will demonstrate that Freud's theory of religion as psychological projection can paradoxically become a vehicle of integration, something the religious believer can use to begin establishing a way to creatively live *within* the dialectical tension that arises anytime one's belief system is challenged and/or disrupted.

Questions to keep in mind throughout this study include the following: Does the believer, who conceives of God and religion as "all good," while avoiding the "all bad" Freudian theory, have a tendency to keep, psychically, the good and bad aspects of self and others far apart? If, along the way, we discover that certain religious believers experience something akin to psychical compartmentalization, when confronted with the all-bad Freud and his

Ricoeur on Freud

all-bad theory of religion as projection, what then? Might there not be, in the face of what initially appears to be a hopeless impasse, an alternative to this either-or framework, a more creative approach that could assist the believer in moving from a dualistic framework to one that is more integrative of aspects of religious faith *and* aspects of Freud's critique of religion? It is my hope that by the end of this book, the religious believer will be able to answer this question in the affirmative.

■ DIFFERENT FIELDS AND DISCIPLINES ■

The *Dictionary of Pastoral Care and Counseling* explicitly states that the full meaning of recent developments within the field of psychoanalysis has yet to be adequately explored by Christian theology, primarily because of Christianity's distaste for anything having to do with Freud. Consequently, I intend to continue the necessary exploration of recent developments within psychoanalysis by bringing together the work of three theorists who have intentionally engaged Freud and his theory of religion. Each of these theorists, in one form or another, argues persuasively and convincingly that the religious believer cannot afford to ignore Freud's work on religion, even if Freud does come to a different conclusion about ultimate reality. I have therefore selected these three theorists for a reason: each of them considers it a mistake to relegate Freud to the periphery, or even beyond the bounds of the discussion on religious faith, particularly when his psychology of religion has been and continues to be so extraordinarily influential. In other words, these three scholars have all adopted a "both-and" stance toward Freud and religion, rather than a dismissive position of "either-or." If we operate from an either-or framework, then one must choose between *either* embracing the totality of religious faith while rejecting the totality of Freudian theory *or* embracing the totality of psychoanalysis while rejecting the totality of religion. One must, so the thinking goes, embrace one or the other: either all of religion or all of Freud. Like oil and water, the two do not and cannot mix.

It is out of this either-or impasse that the theorists can begin leading us. Indeed, these three theorists and their distinct and creative methodologies can be invaluable resources, especially for the religious believer who decides to work *through* rather than *around* the dialectical tension that is sure to develop when his or her belief system is challenged by a Freudian hermeneutics of suspicion. This book, in other words, will not simply be a study of Freud's theory of religion, that is, the study of Freud's psychology of religion will not be an end in itself. While Freud's theory of religion as projection will be a central feature of this book, it will nevertheless serve as the *means* toward the end of establishing a way to creatively live *within* the dialectical tension that develops anytime our faith is confronted by a radically different theory or belief system.

I have already introduced the first theorist, the philosopher and theologian, Paul Ricoeur, who puts forward the idea that a Freudian hermeneutics of suspicion has the capacity, not only to disrupt, but also to purify and enlarge one's religious faith. For example, what the religious believer can learn from, to use Ricoeur's word, the *schooling* of Freud is that an exalted and moralistic God who consoles and protects but also accuses and punishes *is* a projection of the father of childhood in response to our anxiety and helplessness. Whether or not Freud's theory of religion as projection finds scientific and empirical confirmation, Ricoeur is convinced that Freudian psychology, read hermeneutically, confirms that human beings do at times prefer moral condemnation from a punishing God to an existence that is unprotected and unconsoled. However, he is not suggesting, like Freud, that ultimate reality is simply Ananke, "harsh necessity," and that human beings, in the face of this reality, are morally obligated to accept the situation and not pretend it could be otherwise. Through what Ricoeur labels *the grace of imagination*, religious believers can move from the Freudian stance of mere resignation in the face of harsh reality to a more creative mode of dwelling on the earth. Freud, then, according to Ricoeur, is entitled to both a "no" *and* a "yes" from the religious believer. The implication, of course, is that religious believers cannot sidestep Freud, dismissing him outright because he came to an erroneous conclusion about religious faith. It is Ricoeur who will maintain that due to Freud's profound and lasting influence in the West, side-stepping Freud is simply impossible. "[Freud]," writes Ricoeur, "has not only, or even principally introduced a new kind of therapy, but a global interpretation of the phenomenon of culture and of religion as an aspect of culture. Our culture analyzes itself through him—a fact of extreme importance that must be understood and evaluated."[6]

The second theorist, the psychoanalyst Ana-Maria Rizzuto, is convinced that her work in clinical practice demonstrates that our images of God are at least a partial exaltation of parental or early caregiver imagoes. Completely dismissing Freud's theory of religion as psychological projection, therefore, puts clinicians at a disadvantage in their work with patients or clients, as well as clergy in their work with parishioners. Rizzuto even goes so far as to say that our ignorance of God's psychical role in our lives means that we are "missing an important and relevant piece of information" about the developmental history of those in our care.[7] She disagrees, as we will see, with Freud's view that religion is always neurotic or immature or both, but does find his theory particularly helpful and useful when it comes to the psychical juxtaposition of parental imagoes and images of God. Accordingly, Rizzuto believes that if we can focus our attention on Freud's work with psychical experience, instead of immediately citing and disparaging his conclusion about religious faith and ultimate reality, then he has a great deal to teach religious believers about the origin of their images of God.

The third and final theorist, whose work will be foundational for this study, is the feminist scholar of religion, Judith Van Herik. Van Herik engages Freud for reasons other than trying to learn about the human being's willingness to tolerate moral condemnation in exchange for the promise of consolation and protection (Ricoeur) or what psychoanalysis can teach us about psychical images of God (Rizzuto). Instead, Van Herik is more interested in the connection between Freud's theory of religion as projection and his asymmetrical theory of gender. The projective, irrationalist faith of the religious believer (male or female), she argues, and the psychology of women are, in the Freudian view, inextricably linked together through related inner meanings. Religious believers who long for a consoling God to come to them with tender loving care are not very different from women who seem less willing or able than men to renounce ties to parental figures. According to Van Herik, the highest form of human development for Freud is that of *ideal* masculinity, an evolutionary leap in development that would surpass the *normal* masculinity of the present. Ideal masculinity would represent a developmental and renunciatory achievement par excellence, whereby all reality—psychological and ultimate—becomes depersonalized. While Van Herik does admit that Freud sees God as little more than a mental product, and that his views on women's psychology and development were not always charitable, she urges us to return again and again to his work on religion, as well as to his work on gender, in order to discover important clues about Western religio-cultural attitudes. Because Freudianism, if not Freud, has been so influential in the West, particularly in America, "it is important to continue to return to his writings."[8]

■ METHODOLOGY ■

The hermeneutical methodology of Sandra M. Schneiders, the feminist scholar of spirituality and biblical studies, will provide the methodological framework for this book. While Schneiders has specifically applied this particular methodology to the study of Christian spirituality and biblical interpretation, I would argue that it can be a concise and relevant framework for the study of other phenomena, in particular the study of Freud's theory that religious faith is psychological projection. Because of the complex and multifaceted nature of the phenomenon to be studied—religion as psychological projection—this hermeneutical methodology must necessarily be multi- and interdisciplinary.

Schneiders makes the same point when she applies this hermeneutical approach to the study of the equally complex phenomenon of spirituality. She makes the distinction between the study of the subject under investigation in the context of spiritual formation and the study of the same subject in a more research-oriented context. In the former, the emphasis is primarily on the spiritual formation and religious development of the believer, whereas in the latter "the purpose of the study is, as in any research field, the expansion of knowledge in the field."[9] By building on the work of the three theorists—Ricoeur, Rizzuto, and Van Herik—who have intentionally engaged and responded to the Freudian critique of religion, this study will demonstrate that we can do both simultaneously: expand our knowledge of various fields and disciplines *and* emphasize spiritual formation and religious development. Toward this end, the fields of psychology, particularly psychoanalysis and object relations theory, philosophy, theology, and feminist theory will all be in conversation with one another.

Schneiders reminds us that methodology is indeed "metareflection," that is, "a study of the methods that are used to achieve understanding in a particular sphere and of their interrelations."[10] Note that she uses the plural form—*methods*—rather than the singular form—*method*. This, again, reflects Schneiders's conviction that a complex phenomenon, whether it be Christian spirituality, biblical studies, or religious faith as psychological projection, cannot be adequately understood and grasped with only a single method of interpretation. In other words, if we wish to study a complex phenomenon like the origin of religious faith, then the methodology we construct and apply will demand a certain comprehensiveness commensurate with the particular phenomenon. But there is something more than the issue of comprehensiveness, something that also demands a multi- and interdisciplinary methodology: the collapse of "the Cartesian ideal of a single method," which tended to be modeled after the methodology of mathematics and/or the natural or physical sciences. "The collapse of this epistemological ideal," argues Schneiders, and its promise of a unified and universal knowledge, "has necessitated the reopening of the question of method."[11] By reopening the question of method, and by confronting the limitations of any single method of interpretation, we are then in a position to reconstruct a more realistic methodology, a hermeneutical approach that encompasses a multiplicity of different methods of interpretation.

More specifically, Schneiders's hermeneutical approach to a particular phenomenon "involves a triple operation, which is only theoretically sequential since, as the hermeneutical circle revolves, the three phases will mutually condition and recondition each other."[12] The three hermeneutical components of this particular study are as follows: (1) a *description* of the phenomenon under investigation, namely, Freud's theory that religious faith, particularly Judeo-Christian faith or belief in God, is the projection and subsequent objectification of our very own human subjectivity; (2) a *critical analysis* of the phenomenon, by way of Ricoeur, Rizzuto, and Van Herik, who all maintain, in one form or another, that despite his methodological shortcomings and brash and dogmatic conclusions about faith and gender, Freud still has much to teach us about religion in the context of Western culture; and (3) a *constructive interpretation* that takes the research of the phenomenon under investigation beyond mere description and explanation, even beyond critical analysis. The constructive interpretation will be found in the research that demonstrates the hermeneutical value and utility of holding one's religious faith in dialectical tension with psychoanalytic theory, in order to expand, enrich, and ultimately strengthen one's personal faith. In certain ways, this invitation to live within the tension between psychoanalysis and faith resembles the dialectical framework of Paul Tillich, in that dialectic represents "affirmation and negation leading to the discovery of truth, though not necessarily to synthesis."[13]

ONE

Freud's Interpretation of Religion

We live in a world of unreality and dreams. To give up our imaginary position as the center, to renounce it, not only intellectually but in the imaginative part of our soul, that means to awaken to what is real and eternal, to see the true light and hear the true silence.

Simone Weil, *Waiting for God*

I t was Freud's fate, as he himself observed with no shortage of pride and grandiosity, to "agitate the sleep of mankind."[1] While this bold and declarative statement may strike the casual reader of Freud as little more than self-aggrandizement, one could, by taking another look at Freud and at his impact on Western culture, make a compelling case for the fact that it was he, more than any other figure of the twentieth century, who changed the way we think about ourselves as human beings and the way we view human nature. Freud, though, did even more than that: he agitated the sleep of the religious believer, by challenging the believer's conviction that God is in God's heaven and that all is right with the world. The Western world, I would argue, is still trying to come to terms with Freud's influential critique of religion, even now, more than sixty years after his death. Witness the force field of energy emanating from my student in the Religious Conversion class, in response to Freud's theory of religion and to Paul Ricoeur's suggestion that the believer owes Freud at least a partial "yes." The intensity of the student's anger, it would seem, was commensurate with the power of the Freudian critique of religion.

To take this analysis a step further, we could say that this student was trying to come to terms with Freud's critique of religion on multiple levels. In fact, if we apply Freud's first topography of the human psyche—consciousness, preconsciousness, and unconsciousness—to what transpired in the classroom that day, we could say with some precision that this seminarian was trying to come to terms with Freudian theory on three different psychical levels. My lecture on Freud and Ricoeur's interpretation of psychoanalysis

11

jogged this individual's *preconscious* memory of Freud—that is, he could re-call what he had learned or heard of Freud without too much difficulty—which then triggered a *conscious* feeling of anger in response to deeper feelings of an *unconscious* nature. While the latter—unconscious feelings—may appear conjectural, it should be remembered that many theorists and clinicians view anger as a frontline emotion, that which conceals more primitive and threat-ening feelings, such as fear and helplessness. Thus, it is hardly conjectural to suggest that my student, while responding to Freud with conscious anger, was, at an unconscious level, afraid of what psychoanalysis could do to his faith.

What is it, then, about Freud that can still agitate the sleep of religious believers? What is it about his theory of religion that continues to evoke and provoke? Let us take the response of Freud to his friend Romain Rolland, the French writer and philosopher, as our starting point. In 1929, just two years after devoting an entire book—*The Future of an Illusion*—to the issue of religion, Freud made an additional foray into this field of study, in the early portions of another classic book, *Civilization and Its Discontents*. In the very first chapter, Freud tells the reader that Rolland had written to congratulate him upon the successful publication of *The Future of an Illusion*, and that he, Rolland, had agreed with all of Freud's conclusions about religion except one, namely, the origin of "religious sentiments."

Rolland, according to Freud, held the view that these sentiments or feelings of religiosity have their origin in a most distinct and primitive feel-ing, "which he finds confirmed by many others, and which he may suppose is present in millions of people . . . a feeling as of something limitless, un-bounded—as it were, 'oceanic'."[2] Freud was willing to concede that this "oceanic feeling" was present in some, maybe even many people, even though he informed Rolland that the feeling did not ring true to his own personal experience. That Freud could not reconcile the oceanic feeling with his own experience is a fact of no small importance, as we will see when we get to Rizzuto's work. For now, suffice it to keep in mind that Freud, who had years before subjected himself to a period of intense and systematic self-analysis, would not accept as fact something that did not resonate with his own experience. His own experience of religious sentiments or feelings, or, more accurately, the lack thereof, became an important touchstone, consciously and unconsciously guiding his interpretation of religion.

Freud was not entirely inflexible when it came to the matter of the oceanic feeling. Though he says that he had never experienced this primitive longing for the eternal oneness of the universe, it was not beyond the realm of possibility for *other* people to experience it. The only point on which he became inflexible was whether or not the oceanic feeling could be called the "primary source," the *fons et origio* of our religious sentiments. Freud wrote that he had "no right to deny that [the oceanic feeling] does in fact occur in other people. . . . The only question is whether it is being correctly interpreted and whether it ought to be regarded as the *fons et origio* of the whole need for religion."[3] This, of course, was only a rhetorical comment, for by 1929 his mind was already made up on the matter: while some people may experience this oceanic feeling, there is nothing to suggest that it is of a primary nature, that it is the primary source of our religiosity. For one thing, as we have already discovered, Freud could not reconcile the oceanic feeling of oneness with his own personal experience. There was another stumbling block, however, which stood in the way of Freud joining Rolland in support of the oceanic feeling as the origin of religious faith: his theory of the psychosexual development of human beings, and the defining moment of human development, the resolution of the Oedipus Complex.

■ THE DEFINING MOMENT OF DEVELOPMENT ■

According to Freud, when the young child, or, more accurately, the young boy enters the phallic stage of psychosexual development around the age of three, things become rather complicated, both externally, within the family unit, and internally, within the boy's psyche. "The intricacy of the problem," wrote Freud in his defining book, *The Ego and the Id*, "is due to . . . the triangular character of the Oedipus situation. . . ."[4] What Freud had in mind when he wrote of the "triangular character of the Oedipus situation" was the young boy's experience of, and feelings toward, his mother and father. This is the age, so the theory goes, when the boy becomes cognizant of his budding sexuality, the fact that he is a male with a distinct sexual organ. The boy's powerful "object-cathexis for his mother, which originally related to the mother's breast," now takes on genital properties.[5]

He begins to feel "pleasurable sensations in his sexual organ," and learns from firsthand experience that these sensations can be produced at will through the manual stimulation of this organ. At first, the boy's object-cathexis for his mother related solely and uncomplicatedly to her breast. Now, however, the object-cathexis has a sexual quality to it, which undoubtedly makes it more pleasurable, but, at the same time, makes it more frightening. In the boy's internal, object-representational world, "he becomes his mother's lover." Freud goes on to say that

[The boy] wishes to possess [his mother] physically in such ways as he has divined from his observations and intuitions about sexual life, and he tries to seduce her by showing her the male organ which he is proud to own. In a word, his early awakened masculinity seeks to take his father's place with her; his father has hitherto in any case been an envied model to the boy, owing to the physical strength he perceives in him and the authority with which he finds him clothed. His father now becomes a rival who stands in his way and whom he would like to get rid of.[6]

But, getting rid of one's father is easier said than done, especially when one is so young and small. The father, to state the obvious, happens to be bigger and stronger and more powerful. Thus, the young boy, during the oedipal stage of development, is in a state of high anxiety and feels very conflicted. On the one hand, he desperately yearns to become his mother's lover, to possess her physically in new and exciting ways, or, in short, to give free reign to the pleasure principle. Yet, on the other hand, another force is at work in the young boy's psyche, the force of reality or the reality principle, which the external forms and internal images of the father personify. Gone forever is the Edenic state of dyadic oneness and optimal bliss with the mother, when the object-cathexis related solely to her breast. Now, as the object-cathexis becomes more sexualized, the dyadic oneness gives way to a more complicated and triangular pattern of object relations; the father and his imposing presence forcefully enters the picture.

For Rolland and for many others, religious faith represents an attempt to recapture the feeling of Edenic bliss and oneness with the mother, the oceanic feeling one once had in the womb and in the early days and months of life. Freud, though, strongly disagreed with this interpretation. In his view, once the young boy passes through the triangular Oedipus Complex, with all of its pain and fear, he will be forever changed. Religious faith, then, cannot be an attempt to revive the oceanic feeling of oneness with the mother and the universe, for the early state of oneness with the mother is not the defining moment of human development. Since the Oedipus Complex is, and always will be, that defining moment, religious faith can only be the revival or reactivation of the conflicted and ambivalent feelings associated with the oedipal phase of development. Freud was especially unwavering and unyielding on this point: that the oedipal stage of development is the *fons et origio* of the whole need for religious faith is simply nonnegotiable.

Freud's inflexibility on this issue was not just a matter of personality; he had a theoretical rationale for standing firm. When the boy's object-cathexis for his mother related exclusively to the breast, all was fine and good. As the object-cathexis becomes more sexualized, however, the dyadic oneness necessarily gives way to a more complicated pattern of object relations. In wishing to possess his mother, for reasons other than to supply him with physical and emotional nourishment and sustenance, the boy risks losing the love and protection of his father, who is already the mother's lover. "I cannot," Freud argued with conviction, "think of any need in childhood as strong as the need for a father's protection."[7] This, as we will see, underlies his entire theory of religion. While the young boy would love nothing more than to yield to the temptation of the pleasure principle, to indulge his sexual desires by possessing his mother, he is keenly aware that to do so means that the more powerful father becomes his rival rather than his defender. In such a fragile and vulnerable emotional state, the young boy only has one option: the pleasure principle of desire must yield to the reality principle of potential deprivation and retaliation.

During the same period of development—almost as if the illicit wish for the mother and the perceived threat of the father's retaliation were not enough—the young boy makes a startling discovery: there are physical or anatomical differences between the sexes. On the surface, the discovery that boys have a penis and girls do not seems simple enough. And yet, when the discovery is psychically linked with the sexualization of the maternal object-cathexis and with the fear of the loss of paternal protection, the boy becomes even more terrified. Maybe, he begins to speculate, girls initially had a penis, but because of similar illicit and incestuous wishes, they had it taken away from them as punishment. If the boy cannot deny his illicit desires and wishes, then the same fate—the removal of his penis—may also await him. The threat of castration becomes further concretized and more credible, when the boy's mother, in a spirit of disguised playfulness, warns him that she will either take his sexual organ away from him or have his father cut it off, if he does not refrain from touching or fondling it. The boy takes his mother at her word, recalling that she has already taken other cherished things away from him, like her breast and his feces. So, Freud theorizes, "if at the time of the [actual] threat [the boy] can recall the appearance of female genitals or if shortly afterwards he has a sight of them—of genitals, that is to say, which really lack this supremely valued part, then he takes what he has heard seriously and, coming under the influence of the *castration complex*, experiences the severest trauma of his young life."[8]

In an attempt to alleviate or at least to lessen the unbearable feelings of anxiety and fear, the young boy abandons the object-cathexes—mother as desired lover, father as hated rival—of the oedipal period of development and replaces them with an attitude that can best be described as *identification*. The primal fear that he will lose his sexual organ and, simultaneously, his father's protection, prompts the boy to defend himself by way of a reaction formation, to identify with the powerful father by introjecting the father's attitudes and values into his own developing ego. By identifying with the father, the boy is forevermore assured of being loved and protected.

The implications for a critique of religious faith as psychological projection now become more obvious: the boy and the religious believer both fear a supremely powerful father/Father, yet, at the same time, are guaranteed his/His protection. In any case, this attitude of identification with the father's power and authority and the introjection of the father's values signals the resolution of the Oedipus Complex and the formation of the *superego*, the third division of the human psyche, along with the ego and the id. Freud captures the termination of this phase of development with the following remarks, taken from his essay, "The Dissolution of the Oedipus Complex":

> The object-cathexes are given up and replaced by identifications. The authority of the father or the parents is introjected into the ego, and there it forms the nucleus of the super-ego, which takes over the severity of the father and perpetuates prohibitions against incest, and so secures the ego from the return of the libidinal object-cathexis. The libidinal trends belonging to the Oedipus Complex are in part desexualized and sublimated (a thing which probably happens with every transformation into an identification) and in part inhibited in their aim and changed into impulses of affection. The whole process has, on the one hand, preserved the genital organ—has averted the danger of its loss—and, on the other, has paralyzed it—has removed its function. This process ushers in the latency period, which now interrupts the child's sexual development.[9]

Recall that in the beginning, at birth, a child is all *id*, all instinctual energy or, as Freud picturesquely described it, a "cauldron full of seething excitations."[10] In this preoedipal world of existence, the child has no sense of right and wrong, no sense of reality—only pleasure and the immediate gratification of instinctual impulses. It falls to the parents to be, so to speak, the child's temporary conscience, acting in his or her stead until the conscience is more fully developed. But soon enough, children begin to realize for themselves that their parents praise and reward them for certain behaviors, while punishing them for others. The young child's ego, the organizing center of a young and fragile personality, must therefore begin to mediate between the internal and instinctual demands for pleasure and the external demands of reality, as constituted by the parents and the home environment. Little by little, the child introjects or internalizes the norms and standards of the parents, and begins to identify with their values, because, on the one hand, they are more powerful and, on the other hand, they may at any moment withdraw their cherished love and protection. The latter, especially—the perception that the coveted love and protection of one's parents can be lost for failing to meet their standards and expectations—is more than the young child can bear. Indeed, children are filled with feelings of anxiety and fear, which would overwhelm them if it were not for the fact that their developing ego begins to forge something of a middle ground, between the instinctual demands for immediate pleasure and the parental and environmental demands for reality testing.

The parental standards and values, which were external to the child during the preoedipal years of development (age three and under), become internalized during the oedipal phase, particularly with the resolution and the dissolution of the Oedipus Complex. In the early pages of *The Future of an Illusion,* a work that became a systematic discussion and critique of religious faith, Freud stated that

> It is in keeping with the course of human development that external coercion gradually becomes internalized; for a special mental agency, man's super-ego, takes it over and includes it among its commandments. Every child presents this process of transformation to us; only by that means does it become a moral and social being. Such a strengthening of the super-ego is a most precious cultural asset in the psychological field. Those in whom it has taken place are turned from being opponents of civilization into being its vehicles.[11]

In other words, external coercion, applied ever so skillfully and disciplinarily by the earliest representatives of the norms and values of culture, the parents, is psychically transformed into internal repression. The superego, usually at around the age of five—the end of the oedipal stage of development—begins *superego*

to take over the function of authority hitherto carried out by one's parents. What we behold is nothing short of the triumph of culture; the young child is fast becoming a self-regulating member of society. *boy*

In the coming years the child's superego will expand to include the standards and values of other important figures and influences, such as teachers, peers, and religious tradition. Though these later influences are indeed significant in terms of shaping character and personality, they will never be as foundational as the parental images recorded in the psyche. As we have already seen, the trauma resulting from the oedipal period of development and from its association with feelings of fear and helplessness, leaves an indelible and lasting impression in the child's psyche. Because so much, if not all of the oedipal ordeal happened outside the bounds of consciousness— unlike the experiences with the later shapers of personality—the influence of the parents will be uniquely and extraordinarily deep and lasting, of primary importance. The object representations recorded in the psyche during the oedipal period of development ultimately form the bedrock of the superego. As James Strachey has observed, commenting in the preface to Freud's essay, "Mourning and Melancholia," "[Freud] suggested that the very earliest of these regressive identifications—those derived from the dissolution of the Oedipus Complex—come to occupy a quite special position and form, in fact, the nucleus of the super-ego."[12] As we will see shortly, the regressive identifications derived from the dissolution of the Oedipus Complex will also, according to Freud, occupy a special position in the formation of religious faith, forming its nucleus.

For the most part, the superego is "a largely unconscious factor experienced as the conscience."[13] Its function is to supply the ideals and standards by which the ego will mediate between the demands of internal pleasure and those of external reality. Moreover, the superego, in transforming external coercion into a mechanism of internal restraint, takes over the parental function of disciplinarian. It threatens to punish the young child for any illicit actions and behaviors, *as well as* for any illicit thoughts and impulses. The thoughts and impulses, in other words, even if not acted upon, will still be judged with the very same measure of severity. This is an extremely important point to keep in mind, especially when the discussion turns to an omniscient God with the capacity to observe and punish our actions *and* thoughts. For the time being, it is necessary to remember that the superego, by punishing both illicit actions *and* illicit thoughts, will be a harsher disciplinarian than the parents, who only punished the child for improper actions and behaviors. Before the superego had been formed, the young boy could

superego & judgment

not my belief about God

rest assured that as long as he did not *act* upon the erotic impulse to possess his mother and the aggressive impulse to do away with his father, he was innocent before the bar of judgment. Now, he must also guard against the mere *thought* of lust and aggression. In case he ever forgets that the stakes are significantly higher, that he will be judged for what he does, thinks, and feels, the pangs of a guilty conscience will most certainly jog his memory.

The intrapsychic triumph of culture, whereby a child becomes a self-regulating member of society, comes at a high price: the renunciation of one's deepest desires. True, the ego will soon discover that there are plenty of other things in this world from which to derive a certain amount of pleasure and satisfaction. For example, we may, as children or adults, throw ourselves into imaginative play or creative work, sensing that these experiences will bring us a measure of satisfaction and fulfillment. But, as Freud pointed out, the pleasure we derive from any aim-inhibited and socially approved endeavor will always be of a secondary or sublimatory nature. This is the price we pay for becoming contributing members of human society: we must renounce all pleasure of a primary nature, those deepest desires that would bring us the most intense and satisfying pleasure. In a sense, the ego of every individual must eventually come to know its place in the psychical pecking order, recognizing that it will always be held accountable by the introjected standards and values of the culture, as mediated at first by one's parents and later by the superego.

The superego, which we experience psychically as the conscience, can either be a restraining force intended to keep us in check, as in the case of instinctual renunciation, or a motivating force, inciting us to aim ever higher in our pursuit of the introjected parental and cultural ideals. In either case, the superego can be particularly cruel and demanding. When it comes to the former, the renunciation of our deepest desires, Freud, in total agreement with Shakespeare's Hamlet, believed that "conscience does make cowards of us all. . . ."[14] And yet, human individuals really have no other choice, if they wish to live peaceably and harmoniously together in a state of mutual contentment. "I promise to renounce my most basic and primal sexual and aggressive desires, to refrain from harming or taking advantage of you, my neighbor, if you promise to do the same for me," becomes an unspoken pact or agreement necessary for our collective survival.

In Freudian theory, this quid-pro-quo arrangement is the foundation and cornerstone of human civilization. Nevertheless, what we also discover is that no matter how often we live up to the introjected parental and cultural ideals and values, the superego is never satisfied. Genuine and even remarkable achievements and accomplishments on our part may seem to be insignificant and trivial, for before we can even begin to bask in the joy of a job well done, the superego has already begun to demand an even higher and greater state of perfection. Freud found the remark of one of Leonardo da Vinci's students illustrative of this state of affairs, when the superego becomes pathologically rigid and inflexible: "[Leonardo] appeared to tremble the whole time he set himself to paint, and yet he never completed any work he had begun, having so high a regard for the greatness of art that he discovered faults in things that to others seemed miracles."[15]

■ GENDER ASYMMETRY ■

Freud theorized that the young girl, around the same age, also has to work through and resolve a certain set of oedipal issues, that she, too, becomes triangulated in an intricate web of object relations with her mother and father. It is important to note, however, that prior to 1925, Freud had very little to say, explicitly, about the psychology of girls and women. Even after 1925, when he began to deal more systematically with female psychology and sexuality, Freud was, by and large, making sweeping generalizations about female development derived mostly from his research on boys and men.[16] Thus, in the 1920s and 1930s, Freud found himself faced with the daunting challenge of trying to ascertain, in the words of the title of a famous essay, "the anatomical distinction between the sexes." The task seemed rather daunting to Freud because he was applying a masculine theory of human development and sexuality to the study of the sexual life of women, to what he would less than generously refer to as a "dark continent."[17] "Freud," writes Carol Gilligan, "struggled to resolve the contradictions posed for his theory by the differences in female anatomy and the different configuration of the young girl's early family relationships." She continues:

> After trying to fit women into his masculine conception, seeing them as envying that which they missed, he came instead to ac-knowledge, in the strength and persistence of women's pre-Oedipal attachments to their mothers, a developmental difference. He considered this difference in women's development to be respon-sible for what he saw as women's developmental failure.[18]

In Freud's view, what the young girl is bereft and deeply envious of is the male sexual organ. He posited that when the girl discovers that she does not have a penis, she suddenly becomes consumed with very intense feelings of envy, bitterness, and resentment. These powerful feelings are directed at the person perceived to be responsible for this unhappy predicament: the mother. Up until the oedipal period of development, the mother was for the young girl what she was for the young boy, namely, the most primary and most intense object relation. As we have seen, the boy's love for the mother intensifies during this stage of development, only to later be repressed when the hated father becomes too much of a perceived rival and threat.

Unlike the boy, the young girl does not experience an intensification of love for the mother. Rather, she is deeply resentful of her genital disendowment, and holds her mother personally responsible for this physical state of incompleteness. Moreover, the mother's own lack of genital endowment is confirmation of the suspicion that the mother is solely to blame for this unhappy situation. Thus, the young girl experiences, *during* the oedipal period of development, what the young boy will only experience later, at the *end* of the Oedipus Complex: the loosening of the intense and primary relation with the mother as a love-object. Freud, in one of his definitive essays on the psychology of women, writes that "the situation as a whole is not very clear, but it can be seen that in the end the girl's mother, who sent her into the world so insufficiently equipped, is almost always held responsible for her lack of a penis."[19]

The young girl, still smarting from this painful blow to her self-esteem, senses that it is now pointless to look to her mother, or to any other female for that matter, for any meaningful and lasting consolation. Instead, she must, out of necessity, turn her attention in the direction of her father, who alone is in possession of the requisite sexual organ. It is absolutely essential to keep this point in mind, when we turn our attention to Freud's psychology of religion. The young boy, because he is terrified of what the more powerful father might do to him, must turn away from the mother and the hope that she will meet his deepest need for love, affection, and consolation—this he will discover at the *end* of the oedipal period of development. The young girl, however, *already* senses, in the midst of the oedipal conflict, that she cannot turn to the mother for any deep and lasting consolation, because the mother is the source of the girl's pain and bitter disappointment. Therefore, the girl looks to the father for compensatory satisfaction, sensing that although he cannot give her a penis—that is, cannot turn her into a boy—he can at least, as he has done with the mother, give her a penis-substitute, in the form of a baby. Already, we can begin to see the handwriting on the wall, that which will prompt Freud to conclude, "Psycho-analysis has made us familiar with the intimate connection between the father-complex and belief in God; it has shown us that a personal God is, psychologically, nothing other than an exalted father."[20]

According to Freud, both boys and girls pass through this triangularly complicated pattern of object relations, known as the Oedipus Complex, roughly between the ages of three and five. And both boys and girls, during this pivotal stage of development, struggle to come to terms with the new and powerfully intense feelings they experience vis-à-vis their parents. But, this is about as far as the similarities go. One could try to make a case for the issue of castration, as an additional point of commonality between the Oedipus Complex of the boy and that of the girl—in both cases, it is a pivotal developmental factor. Yet, while the young boy and the young girl both experience a castration complex, they experience it in decisively different ways. Castration, for the boy, is a perceived threat, something he dreads and lives in fear of, whereas for the girl castration is something she has always and will always have to live with, a fait accompli. To put this more succinctly, the crucial ingredient missing from the young girl's oedipal conflict, something she does not share with the boy, is the anticipatory dread of castration. "The difference," writes Freud, "between the sexual development of males and females at the stage we have been considering is an intelligible consequence of the anatomical distinction between their genitals and the psychical situation involved in it; it corresponds to the difference between a castration that has been carried out and one that has merely been threatened."[21]

One cannot overestimate the importance of this difference, between the anticipatory dread of castration and castration as an accomplished fact, for Freud and his theory of gender. The same, as we will soon see, is equally true of Freud and his psychology of religion. The young boy, terrified of being castrated for harboring erotic and aggressive desires, has no choice but to urgently identify with, and introject the values and standards of, his parents. The young girl, on the other hand, lacking a similar anticipatory dread of castration, does not have the same sense of urgency to introject the values of her parents. Since these introjected values of parents and culture become the bedrock and very essence of the child's superego, it only stands to reason that the girl's superego will be weaker and less developed than the boy's. When it comes to the girl's Oedipus Complex, then, the motivation for its dissolution—castration anxiety—is lacking. Unlike the situation of the boy, where we see the Oedipus Complex, as Freud puts it, "smashed to pieces by the shock of threatened castration," the Oedipus Complex, for the girl, "escapes the fate which it meets with in boys: it may be slowly abandoned or dealt with by repression, or its effects may persist far into women's normal mental life."[22] This lack of finality, the fact that the girl's Oedipus Complex has not been smashed to pieces or has not reached a definitive and decisive end, but has instead persisted well into adulthood, simply provides Freud with additional "data" supporting the view that the woman's superego is less developed.

But what, exactly, does it mean to have a weaker and less developed superego? Freud explains it this way:

> I cannot evade the notion (though I hesitate to give it expression) that for women the level of what is ethically normal is different from what it is in men. The super-ego is never so inexorable, so impersonal, so independent of its emotional origins as we require it to be in men. Character-traits which critics of every epoch have brought up against women—that they show less sense of justice than men, that they are less ready to submit to the great exigencies of life, that they are more often influenced in their judgments by feelings of affection or hostility—all these would be amply accounted for by the modification in their super-ego. . . .[23]

Thus, when it comes to the matter of ethics, morality, and values, the male, according to Freud, is in a position to take the lead, to make sounder judgments more independent of feelings and emotions. Freud, of course, was betraying his rationalistic bias, that the impersonal logic and reason of the male is inherently more valuable and carries more weight than the personal feelings and emotions of women. Consequently, in the social arena, only the opinions of those individuals in possession of a depersonalized superego that is rationally aligned with the standards of culture can be trusted and respected.

What is unfortunate, in terms of Freud's psychosexual theory of development and his conclusions about gender, is that he "painted" with excessively broad brushstrokes: women, who have less moral sense, who are ruled more by their emotions than their intellect, can only "inherit" their morality and values from men. We can already sense where Freud is headed when he takes his next logical and theoretical step: women, in possession of an underdeveloped superego, who must get their morality and values from men, the bearers of a more evolved superego, must, through a similar process of cross-inheritance, get their religion from men. Who, after all, yearns the most for the love and protection of an exalted father/Father? Answer: the male, who almost lost his father's love and protection, if not for the threat of castration.

Freud was well aware of the fact, even in 1925, that various critics were noticing that his psychology of women was formulated from a distinctly masculine point of view. Nevertheless, and this had become something of a recurring pattern, Freud was immovable, unable or unwilling to hear any constructive criticism regardless of the soundness of the opposing argument. For someone who, at least in theory, valued and prized reason and logic above everything else, it is rather ironic that Freud refused to listen to reason, especially with issues that certainly demanded a second look. This, to repeat, was something of a pattern with Freud, something that both supporters and critics alike could expect without fail.

Freud's classic inflexibility can also be seen in his work with phylogenetics, the study of the evolution of the human species, and particularly his unwavering acceptance of Lamarckian theory, the view that human beings are born into this world with inherited or acquired characteristics or traits. In his 1918 paper on the Wolf Man ("From the History of an Infantile Neurosis"), arguably his most famous case study, Freud wrote that "I cannot feel surprised that what was originally produced by certain circumstances in prehistoric times and was then transmitted in the shape of a predisposition to its re-acquirement should, since the same circumstances persist, emerge once more as a concrete event in the experience of the individual."[24] This would have been all well and good, if it were not for the fact that even in 1918 biologists, in a spirit of virtual unanimity, had already discredited the Lamarckian theory as untenable. Yet, true to form, Freud would not listen to reason.

While it is not too difficult for those of us living today to see that the Lamarckian theory of inherited traits or characteristics may have important implications for the present study of genetics, it must be remembered that in Freud's day there were few if any good scientific reasons for accepting this theory. Freud, though, remained unfazed. He stubbornly refused to part with this portion of his theory—human beings are born with inherited characteristics—even in the face of overwhelming evidence to the contrary. Peter Gay, the Freud biographer, puts it this way:

> We encounter here . . . one of Freud's most eccentric and least defensible intellectual commitments: Freud accepted a version of the Lamarckian doctrine—most probably encountered in the writings of Darwin, who himself subscribed to that theory in part—that acquired characteristics (in [the case of the Wolf Man] the "memory" of being seduced in childhood or being threatened with castration) can be inherited. Few reputable biologists of the

time were willing to credit, and few analysts felt at all comfortable with, this thesis. But Freud stayed with it.[25]

In spite of overwhelming evidence that seemingly contradicted Lamarckianism, Freud clung tenaciously to this theory of inherited traits, not because he had other scientific findings that were more conclusive but because he was unwilling to consider any research that might contradict the theory of psychoanalysis. Similarly, when his psychology of women was challenged for its obvious oversights and shortcomings, Freud was equally unyielding. Karen Horney, a contemporary of Freud, and a psychoanalyst, had, as Freud would have known, "asserted a model of women with positive primary feminine qualities and self-valuation, against Freud's model of woman as defective and forever limited." Furthermore, Horney had tied "her critique of both psychoanalytic theory and women's psychology to her recognition of a male-dominant society and culture."[26] Still, while acknowledging and even commending the work of the women analysts of his day, Freud, commenting on the female superego, argued that "we must not allow ourselves to be deflected from such conclusions by the denials of the feminists, who are anxious to force us to regard the sexes as completely equal in position and worth. . . ."[27] One could paraphrase Gay and say that although Freud sensed that at the time a growing number of women analysts felt uncomfortable with his psychology of female development, he characteristically clung to it just as he had the Lamarckian theory, refusing to modify it by including the findings of respected colleagues.

At this point, it may appear as if there is plenty of justification for abandoning this study of Freudian theory.[28] Freud, it is true, did not always have the most flattering things to say about women. Nor did he attach much importance to the role of women in the development of cultural standards, morals, and values. When Freud, for example, identifies the Oedipus Complex as the origin of religious values and feelings, make no mistake, he is describing the *masculine reactivation* of the Oedipus Complex. The male, with a more developed superego, will play the primary role in the formation of religious faith. As in the case of morality and a sense of justice, the woman will get her religion from the more psychically endowed male, through the process of cross-inheritance. Indeed, there are probably those who wonder why anyone would want to engage Freudian theory more extensively, especially after seeing the way in which he undervalues the psyche of women. Nor is the undervaluation of the psyche limited to women; religious believers, male and female, will receive the same treatment.

We could, quite naturally, simply attribute the undervaluation of female psychology to context, to the time and place in which Freud was living. Freud, as Gay has observed, was hardly alone in conferring on women a second-class status: "Freud was an unreconstructed nineteenth-century gentleman. . . . He never adjusted his old-fashioned manners to a new age. . . ."[29] Maybe, but that is not all. As Philip Rieff has pointed out, one cannot excuse Freud's view of women simply on the grounds that it reflects the "culture-prejudice" of his day and age:

> A denial of the Freudian psychology of women cannot depend on historical reductions of Freud's own psychology. It is not enough to say that Freud himself reproduced the "masculine protest" characteristic of his time and place. His misogyny, like that of his predecessors, is more than prejudice; it has a vital intellectual function in his system.[30]

As it stands, we can join one group of feminists and flatly refuse to engage Freud and his theory of gender, because it is, in the opinion of this group, a misogynistic psychology *of* women, devoted to the devaluation of women. Or, we can follow another group of feminists, the group that sees Freud as having constructed a theory *about* women, a theory which, in the words of Judith Van Herik, "shows how gender is humanly produced." Van Herik goes on to say that "what differentiates those who . . . reject Freudian psychology as harmful to women from those who . . . use Freudian theory for feminist purposes is that the latter judge Freud to have created a theory *about* gender asymmetry as well as a gender-asymmetrical theory."[31] The latter group of feminists, then, adopts a both-and approach to Freudian theory.

To be sure, Freud does in fact deduce from his research that women are less psychically endowed, yet he takes umbrage at his colleague Ernest Jones's suggestion that women are simply *born*, affirming instead that women, to a great extent, are *made* in a particular cultural milieu. Thus, psychoanalytic theory is resistant to our attempts at situating it in a particular pigeonhole. Van Herik, in chapter 4, will make explicit connections between Freud's theory of gender and his psychology of religion. But before getting to the work of the theorists, we must first turn our attention to Freud's psychology of religion proper, which, as we will see, emerges quite naturally from his theory of the Oedipus Complex and the formation of the superego.

■ THE NEED FOR RELIGION ■

As we turn our attention to Freud's theory of religion, we are immediately confronted by a striking paradox. Freud, on the one hand, always spoke disapprovingly of religious faith, dismissing it as inefficacious in the life of the individual and an impediment to the evolution of the human species. And yet, on the other hand, he could not, to his dying day, stop thinking and writing about religion. Indeed, try as best he may, Freud could not banish the thought of religion from his mind. Significant quantities of time and energy were devoted to the study of this "irrelevant" subject, leading to the publication of three books dealing exclusively with the origin of religion (*Totem and Taboo*, *The Future of an Illusion*, and *Moses and Monotheism*), other books dealing with religion in part (e.g., *Civilization and Its Discontents*), and numerous essays and letters dealing with the issue of religion either in full or in part. Ana-Maria Rizzuto will have more to say about this paradox when we get to her work in chapter 3. She will argue that a knowledge of Freud's personality, to the extent we are familiar with it, is a fundamental prerequisite to understanding his theorizing on religion.

For now, suffice it to say that Freud's head and heart were split over the issue of religion: while his head and his intellect told him that religious faith was irrelevant or passé, his heart and emotions were telling him something entirely different. Confirmation of this internal "split" or tug-of-war, manifested in Freud's seeming dismissal of religion and his lifelong preoccupation with it, can be seen in Rizzuto's remarkable discovery that "the chronological study of all Freud's writings, from correspondence to published works, reveals that biblical citations occur in most of them and that Freud cites the Bible more frequently than any other source. . . ."[32]

What became the central feature of Freud's psychology of religion was that a personal God is nothing more than an exalted father. Freud was convinced that a most intimate connection exists, psychically, between an individual's father-complex and his or her belief in God. In fact, the two, at bottom, are inseparable if not indistinguishable. Freud's bold and declarative statement, that "a personal God is nothing other than an exalted father," can be found in his book on Leonardo da Vinci, written in 1910, but even as early as 1901 he had already concluded that the familiar biblical tenet, "God created man in His own image," should be reversed: "Man created God in his."[33] This tenet in reverse was recorded in the popular book, *The Psychopathology of Everyday Life*, which gives even the casual reader of psychoanalysis enough indication of where Freud is headed with his critique of religion. By the end of the book, Freud deduces that the whole history of mythology and religion, including "the myths of paradise and the fall of man, of God, of good and evil, of immortality," can be summed up with a single interpretative word: *projection*. The religious faith of believers, so it seems, amounts to "nothing but psychology projected into the external world...."[34] And what, exactly, are human beings projecting out onto the Rorschachian screen of the universe? Freud, in his book on da Vinci, would be more specific: a personal God is, psychologically, nothing other than the projection of an exalted image of one's earthly father.

But what would make human individuals project a psychical representation of the earthly father of childhood into the heavens, creating in their minds an image of a heavenly Father that bears a striking resemblance to an earthly father? For Freud, there is but one answer: human helplessness. As children, we long for the day when we will reach adulthood and, like our parents and other adults, be free of the feelings of helplessness and powerlessness. However, as adults know only too well, the feelings of helplessness and powerlessness do not suddenly and magically disappear with the cessation of childhood. True, the fear and turmoil associated with the oedipal period of development is now a thing of the past, yet, with the advent of adolescence and subsequent adulthood, individuals soon discover that new dangers await them, dangers that are every bit as unsettling as the threat of castration. It was Shakespeare who, by way of King Lear, reminded us that we human beings, from the day of our birth to the day of our death, are the "poor naked wretches ... that bide the pelting of this pitiless storm."[35] For the adult, the pitiless storm of the Oedipus Complex, with its accompanying castration anxiety, may have subsided, but now there are new storms that seem infinitely more complicated and threatening. What adults must eventually come to terms with is that something ominous could be lurking around the proverbial corner, like an earthquake or flood, a disease or illness, economic misfortune, or even death itself.

At the end of the Oedipus Complex, it seemed as if the all-powerful father would be able to meet the young boy's need for safety and security, for the duration of his life. All the boy had to do was abandon the erotic desire to possess the mother and the aggressive desire to eliminate the father, then introject or internalize the parental standards and values, and he would receive his father's lifetime guarantee of protection. But before too long the child begins to sense that the earthly father is not omnipotent, that the father cannot shield the child from every single threat and danger. Consequently, to recover the fleeting feeling of security, the child must begin to image a more powerful protector and defender, a defender who is necessarily *supra*human. This process of reimaging is similar to the psychical transition that occurs near the end of the oedipal period of development. The child, during the first few years of life, feels safe and secure in the presence of the mother; she is, as it were, the child's initial protection and defense against the dangers of life. Freud observed that

> In this way the mother, who satisfies the child's first hunger, becomes its first love-object and certainly also its first protection against all the undefined dangers which threaten it in the external world—its first protection against anxiety, we may say. In this function [of protection] the mother is soon replaced by the stronger father, who retains that position for the rest of childhood.[36]

According to Freud, once the threat and/or reality of castration enters the developmental picture, the child, male or female, will need to identify with someone more powerful than the mother, someone with the capacity to defend the child against even greater dangers. That someone, of course, is the "stronger father," who, in Freud's words, "retains that position for the rest of childhood." Freud, it must be remembered, always chose his words with the greatest care and precision. When he writes that the stronger father, following the oedipal period, retains the position of protector and defender for the rest of childhood, Freud means just that—for the rest of *childhood*, but not for the rest of one's life. When the great danger of life was the threat of diminished nourishment, the mother was powerful enough to be the child's defender. Then, when the child was faced with a more menacing danger—castration—the psychical image of the mother as protector gave way, out of necessity, to that of the stronger father. Later, when the dangers become even greater, when the threats and storms of adult life suddenly seem of cosmological proportion, the once-powerful father suddenly appears rather diminutive, if not pitiable.

What is needed in the face of graver threats and dangers, like natural disasters, illness, and death is even greater protection and solace, more than an earthly father can supply. We are forced to look beyond our family, even beyond the human race, to a suprahuman divine Power, or, as Freud put it, to "a benevolent Providence which is only seemingly stern and will not suffer us to be a plaything of the overmighty and pitiless forces of nature."[37] This benevolent Providence, psychically molded in the image of its predecessor, the earthly father, is subsequently transformed into a stronger and

more exalted Defender, who takes over the function of protection. To sum-
marize, when it comes to the psychical function of protection, the mother of
the preoedipal years is replaced by the stronger father of the oedipal years
who himself is replaced by an even stronger benevolent Providence, who
retains that position for the rest of the individual's life.

Paul Ricoeur, as we will see in chapter 2, argues that Freud is most
convincing when he links the need for religion with the feeling of perpetual
helplessness. In fact, Ricoeur goes so far as to say that anytime human individuals willingly subject themselves to the accusations and chastisements of
an exacting Providence, their personal God, in this particular instance, *is*
little more than the exalted father of the Oedipus Complex. To put this
another way, Freudian theory, according to Ricoeur, has quite a bit of explanatory or interpretative power, anytime the human individual tolerates or
even gladly accepts the moral condemnation of a punishing God instead of
facing an existence that is unprotected and unconsoled. The only problem
is that Freud extends this interpretation across the board, as if every religious
believer is somehow arrested, emotionally and spiritually, at the oedipal stage
of development. We cannot help but be puzzled at how Freud could unilat-
erally assume that the danger of castration, from which we need a father's
protection, is infinitely more threatening than the danger of diminished
nourishment and sustenance, which we first receive from a mother.

To return to Rolland's point, might not religious faith represent, at certain times, something of a regression to a *pre*oedipal stage of development, to
that oceanic feeling of universal oneness with the mother when we were
physically and emotionally nourished by a single source? If so, religious faith
would then represent, at least in part, either a regression to the state of original
oneness with the preoedipal mother or a regression to the psychical space
between the "me" and the "not me," otherwise known as the transitional
space. As object relations theorists, including Rizzuto, maintain, either way the
psychological roots of religious faith are *not* in the oedipal period of development. Moreover, if it is established that an individual's religious faith has a
preoedipal origin, we would need to determine if that faith is the manifestation
of a *healthy* regression or the return to a more unified state of existence that
preceded the turbulent and fragmentizing years of oedipal development.

In any case, it was Freud's firm conviction that "biologically speaking,
religiousness is to be traced to the small human child's long-drawn-out helplessness and need of help; and when at a later date he perceives how truly
forlorn and weak he is when confronted with the great forces of life, he feels
his condition as he did in childhood, and attempts to deny his own despon-

religious actions as neurotic

dency by a regressive revival of the forces which protected his infancy."[38] If we delineate our study to this particular quote, taken from the pages of Freud's analysis of da Vinci, then we could say with a reasonable degree of certainty that classical psychoanalysis and object relations theory are not too far apart. However, when the "regressive revival" relates to, as Freud saw it, the reactivation of *paternal* forces in every time and place, then he and object relations theorists, like Rizzuto, must go their separate ways.

Freud was not content to leave the matter there, for his audience might be tempted to conclude that while he did in fact suggest that a psychical connection exists between an earthly father and a heavenly Father, it is really left to the individual believer to determine if that connection is a healthy one or not. Seeing this coming, Freud proceeded to launch something of a preemptive strike: anytime individuals, in the face of the pitiless storms of life, revive the forces that protected their infancy and childhood, this regressive revival is always an immature and neurotic psychical maneuver. The connection between the religious practices of the believer and the obsessive actions of the neurotic individual—both of these being, at bottom, immature and childish regressions to the emotional world of infancy and childhood—can be seen very clearly in Freud's paper of 1907, "Obsessive Actions and Religious Practices." Freud, with uncharacteristic modesty, pointed out that "I am certainly not the first person to have been struck by the resemblance between what are called obsessive actions in sufferers from nervous affections and the observances by means of which believers give expression to their piety."[39]

Certainly, the term *obsession* or *obsessional idea* (*Zwangsvorstellung*) had been batted around in medical and psychological circles for some time prior to the publication of this particular paper. But it is Freud who put forward the psychoanalytic term and concept, *Zwangsneurose*, which literally means "obsessional neurosis."[40] *Zwangsneurose*, Freud believed, could be applied, diagnostically and interchangeably, to both compulsive thinking *and* religious actions and practices. Note that with the former, it is not thinking in general, but *compulsive* thinking in particular that happens to be neurotic. In terms of the latter, however, it is religious actions and practices in general—in any shape or form—that Freud diagnoses as neurotic.

What could embolden Freud to make such a brash and daring pronouncement? The answer to that question comes from the clinical data of psychoanalysis. Freud was convinced that there were incontrovertible parallels between what he called the "ceremonials" of his neurotic patients and the ceremonials or rituals of religious believers. "Both actions, he says, are carried out with scrupulous attention to every detail; they are conducted in *rituals*

is it neorotic behavior?

isolation from all other activities and brook no interruption; and their neglect is followed by anxiety or guilt."[41] Ricoeur, when we get to chapter 2, will have more to say about the "scrupulous conscience," which devotes more attention and energy to minutiae than to the important matters of life and religious faith. For now, it is important to keep in mind that, for Freud, the ceremonials and rituals of neurotics and religious believers have a common origin, namely, the regressive revival of the forces of infancy and childhood in the face of life's pressures and disappointments.

The parental—that is, paternal—forces, once external to the child, are now internal to the adult, experienced psychically as images and representations of assurance, protection, and consolation. But while the individual may feel, as a result of this psychical framework, a measure of comfort and security, the feeling comes at a substantial price: perpetual infantilization. Most human beings, Freud believed, would gladly accept infantilization and neuroticism if it means not having to grow up into reality. He was not oblivious to the fact that others, even respected friends (e.g., the Swiss pastor, Oskar Pfister), saw more of a difference between the ceremonials of the neurotic person and the rituals and practices of the religious believer. For example, while the neurotic compulsively performs his or her ceremonials in private, the believer, by and large, observes and performs the rituals of religious faith publicly or en masse, in the company of other religious believers. Moreover, while neurotic ceremonials are narcissistic in nature, meaningful to the neurotic alone, the rituals of religious faith direct the community of believers outward toward a divine and transcendent reality. Freud would have agreed that certain theologians and members of the clergy might make this distinction, but to the *ordinary* believer, religious rituals are performed for less impressive reasons.

Chief among these reasons is that protection and consolation will follow from worshiping and serving God. Most believers, in other words, harbor some form of neurotic anxiety, fearing that if they offend God they will automatically lose God's love and protection. Similarly, the neurotic's obsessive "beliefs" and "rituals" function as a defense against feelings of fear and helplessness. Specifically, the neurotic fears that he or she may act upon a primitive sexual or aggressive impulse, and therefore performs certain obsessive actions as a defense against the forbidden impulse or action. "In the course of the repression of this instinct," Freud observed in "Obsessive Actions and Religious Practices," "a special *conscientiousness* is created which is directed against the instinct; but this psychical reaction-formation feels insecure and constantly threatened by the instinct which is lurking in the unconscious." Freud continues:

The influence of the repressed instinct is felt as a temptation, and during the process of repression itself anxiety is generated, which gains control over the future in the form of expectant anxiety. The process of repression which leads to obsessional neurosis must be considered as one which is only partly successful and which increasingly threatens to fail. It may thus be compared to an unending conflict; fresh psychical efforts are continually required to counterbalance the forward pressure of the instinct. Thus the ceremonial and obsessive actions arise partly as a defense against the temptation and partly as a protection against the ill which is expected.[42]

In this brief (a mere eleven pages), yet pivotal essay, Freud fired something of a "warning shot," giving the reader a clear idea of what is to come when the subject of religion is discussed more systematically. In many ways, it is nothing short of a revolutionary idea: "The formation of a religion, too, seems to be based on the suppression, the renunciation, of certain instinctual impulses."[43] Keep in mind that "Obsessive Actions and Religious Practices" was written in 1907, two decades before the publication of *The Future of an Illusion*. This, no doubt, accounts for Freud inserting the phrase, "seems to be," into what is already a provocative statement. In 1907, even though he had made up his mind on the matter of religion, Freud was more diplomatic, still courting, to some extent, the favor and respect of friend *and* foe. When he publishes *The Future of an Illusion*, there will be no holding back: the formation of religion *is* based on instinctual renunciation. Just as the neurotic fears losing control of sexual or aggressive impulses, so, too, the religious believer fears giving in to the temptation to indulge similar desires, or the temptation to ignore his or her duty to God and neighbor.

Freud was convinced that it is not a coincidence that the believer's humble plea, "And lead us not into temptation," is central to religious faith in the West. As Freud noted with the neurotic, a special conscientiousness and/or sense of guilt arises and is directed at the instinctual or egoistic impulse and temptation. But, just like the neurotic, the psychical reaction formation only feels partially and temporarily successful. Due to "an expectant anxiety in the form of divine punishment,"[44] it becomes absolutely necessary to ritualize the taming of instinctual and egoistic impulses. Freud, at this point, took the argument even further, to its logical conclusion, announcing, with words that are now very familiar, that "in view of the similarities and analogies one might venture to regard obsessional neurosis as a pathological counterpart of the formation of a religion, and to describe that neurosis as an individual religiosity and religion as a universal obsessional neurosis."[45]

It is important to note that Freud inserted the word, *universal,* before the term, *Zwangsneurose,* or "obsessional neurosis." Why, we might be tempted to ask, did Freud not write that neurosis is a religion and religion is a neurosis, and leave it at that? If anything, in the interest of precision and clarity, it would have made better sense to limit the field of observation and study to a *single* context, either individual *or* universal. In other words, if we did not know any better, we might conclude that from a methodological standpoint, Freud's paper, "Obsessive Actions and Religious Practices," was a sloppy piece of work. It would seem that Freud would have been further ahead if he had written, "Obsessional neurosis is an individual religiosity and religion is an *individual* neurosis." This, at least, would have enhanced the possibility that his research was methodologically sound. Besides, up until this time, the data in support of the linking together of neurosis and religion had come exclusively from Freud's clinical treatment of *individual* patients.

How, then, can Freud suggest that data from clinical work with individuals can suddenly be applied universally to another subject of investigation? Recall that Freud always selected his words with the greatest care and precision. The decision, therefore, to link the private religiosity of the neurotic with the universal neurosis of religious faith signals an important shift in Freud's thought, one that becomes even more apparent with the publication of the controversial work, *Totem and Taboo.* Freud, it cannot be emphasized enough, was not satisfied to agitate the sleep of an individual religious believer or two. Rather, he wanted to agitate the sleep of all religious believers, if not the sleep of the entire human race.

■ RELIGION'S PRIMITIVE BEGINNINGS ■

With the publication of *Totem and Taboo,* in 1913, Freud shifted his methodological focus from ontogenetics to that of phylogenetics, from the study of the human individual, and that person's unique developmental history, to the study of the history and evolution of the human species. Freud, as he did with his clinical patients, was working his way back to the beginning, to the primordial beginnings of the human race. And what, exactly, did he find, as a result of this "archaeological" investigation? Modern individuals, he argued, contrary to popular wisdom, are not as psychologically differentiated

submission to ceremony ritual

from their primitive ancestors as they would like to believe. In fact, as Freud explained at the very beginning of *Totem and Taboo*, "a comparison between the psychology of primitive peoples, as it is taught by social anthropology, and the psychology of neurotics, as it has been revealed by psycho-analysis, will be bound to show numerous points of agreement and will throw new light upon familiar facts in both sciences."[46]

Freud was linking the psychology of primitive peoples with the psychology of the modern neurotic individual (the dominant personality type of his day), which, keeping in mind his earlier comparison of neurosis and religious faith, can only be taken to its logical conclusion: *prehistoric man*, to use Freud's term, psychologically resembles the modern neurotic who psychologically resembles the modern religious believer. It would appear that there are no appreciable degrees of psychological separation between the primitive individual, the neurotic, and the religious believer. Religious faith and obsessional neurosis both hark back to common and humble beginnings.

What Freud discovered in his study of totemism was that primitive individuals, neurotics, and religious believers all share a common psychical feature: submission to particular ceremonials or rituals. These rituals function to keep individuals defended against the temptation to give free reign to primal impulses and against the punishment and misfortune that would necessarily result from yielding to temptation. This common feature, at bottom, is really an escape from the real world of material reality into a world of fantasy, which can then be controlled and managed through the power of magical thinking. Freud traced the evolution of this "omnipotence of thoughts" from the infancy of the human race to the present: in the beginning, or at the *animistic stage* of human evolution, human beings overvalued their own psychical processes, believing there was a one-to-one correspondence between thinking a thought and its subsequent manifestation in the external world. For example, if a primitive person harbored secret thoughts about the death of a neighbor, and that neighbor suddenly dies, even from natural causes or from old age, the primitive person would instinctively believe he or she caused the neighbor's demise. Later, in the *religious stage* of human evolution (the stage of the present day and age), human beings project the omnipotence of their own thoughts onto the gods or God: if my neighbor dies it is not because I thought it or wished it, but rather because God willed it or caused it to happen. However, human beings, even in the religious stage of evolution, retain a certain measure of omnipotent thinking for themselves, believing that through the "magic" of prayer they can persuade the gods or God to spare the neighbor's life.

Freud, very much under the influence of Enlightenment thinking, hoped that the human species was on the doorstep of a third stage of development, namely, the *scientific stage* of human evolution, which would involve a decrease in fantasy and an increase in reality, a subordination of the pleasure principle to the reality principle. The age of science, Freud believed, would take us further than we have ever been before, beyond the stages of animism and religion. The two—animism and religion—are intimately linked together through the phenomenon of magical thinking: "Animism is the first system of thought in which we see a shift away from an unsatisfying and ungovernable reality into an altogether more pleasurable world of fantasy, in which reality seems less alien because it can to an extent be controlled by the ceremonials of magic." Michael Palmer goes on to say that

> Herein lies animism's connection to religion. Religion continues the same movement away from the real world, and in the practices of religion we see much the same flight into fantasy. To call religion, therefore, a universal obsessional neurosis is to do more than ally it with certain mental disturbances: it is to reveal part of its own historical foundation, animism, and to conceive of it therefore as another example of how the omnipotence of thought—the primary mechanism of obsessional neurosis—operates. Religion is the child of animism, in other words, not merely because it inherits the belief that spiritual beings exist—an ideal which, according to Freud, underlies all religious belief—but also because it applies magical arts for the control of nature and the appeasement of spiritual powers, now externalized in the form of gods. Religion thus stands as a form of superstition, and obsessional religious acts as acts of magic: they become, as it were, the modern ritual equivalents of the ceremonials of animism, with their prohibitions, precautions, expiations, and substitute satisfactions.[47]

Freud, however, would not stop there. He would not be content until he had pieced together the entire primordial history of the human species. That history, he thought, could be elicited through the careful study of totemism. In putting forth his reconstruction of totemism, Freud drew primarily from the writings and findings of natural scientists, anthropologists, and biblical scholars, including, respectively, Charles Darwin, James Frazier and Robertson Smith. Primitive human beings, according to Darwinian history, lived in small groups or "hordes" ruled by a single, powerful male leader who happened to be violently possessive of the women in his group. Indeed, to maintain his hold on *all* the women of the tribe, this powerful and jealous male leader proceeded to drive out and/or kill all male rivals. "One day," wrote Freud, "the brothers who had been driven out came together, killed and devoured their father and so made an end of the patriarchal horde."[48] On the one hand, the brothers had solved the problem of being dominated by a tyrannical leader. Unfortunately, they had created another problem for themselves, one that would prove to be infinitely more complicated: they now felt guilty.

The problem, as it were, had gone underground, from "out there" in the external person of the tribal patriarch to "in here" in the brothers' psyche, in the form of a sense of guilt. The band of brothers, just like the young boy of the Oedipus Complex, harbored conflicted feelings toward the more powerful father. They resented his authority and power, yet, simultaneously, longed to be just like him. He was their rival, but also their ideal, and now he was gone and his blood was on their hands. To assuage their feelings of remorse over the guilty deed, the brothers banded together into a more cohesive clan, and began to marry *outside* the clan or tribe. They, in other words, "turned to the practice of exogamy—thereby removing the original motive for killing their father—and created a father-substitute in the form of the totem. The yearly celebration of the totem meal was, accordingly, nothing less than the solemn commemoration of the original crime, the murder of the father."[49] Furthermore, in eating together the sacrificed totem animal, a direct substitute for the murdered father, the brothers could identify with the father and consequently acquire a measure of his strength and power. One can immediately see the parallels between this particular interpretation of totemism and the Sacrament of the Lord's Supper.

We now can plainly see the handwriting on the wall: phylogeny is always present in ontogeny. To be even more precise, the Oedipus Complex of the human individual always recapitulates the Oedipus Complex of the human race. The young boy's sense of guilt, stemming from the erotic impulse to possess the mother and the aggressive impulse to do away with the father, corresponds directly to the brothers' sense of guilt over the killing of the father and their wish to possess the women of the horde. True, the original patricidal crime was an actual historical event (this is how Freud saw it), while the incestuous and murderous crimes of the modern-day Oedipus Complex are only enacted in fantasy. To Freud, who had already theorized about the power of magical thinking or the omnipotence of thoughts in the context of his discussion on obsessional neurosis and religious faith, it really made little difference. For the young boy of the present, to think is to act, so that fantasizing about possessing the mother and eliminating the father fills him with a sense of guilt no less real than that of the brothers of the primal horde.

Freud, at this point, in suggesting that ontogeny recapitulates phylogeny, was presupposing that the Lamarckian theory of inherited traits or characteristics still holds true. And while we today might find parallels between Lamarckianism and the present-day study of genetics, biologists of Freud's day had unanimously discredited the inherited-traits theory, to the extent that there was little reason to hold to it. Freud did admit, in *Moses and Monotheism*, that "my position, no doubt, is made more difficult by the present attitude of biological science, which refuses to hear of the inheritance of acquired characteristics by succeeding generations." Nevertheless, in characteristic fashion, Freud pressed on, writing that "I must, however, in all modesty, confess that nevertheless I cannot do without this factor in biological evolution."[50] Not that Freud was being a visionary in terms of any future debate having to do with Lamarckianism and genetics; he knew where *he* stood on the matter, and that was where he was determined to leave it. Moreover, by the time he reaffirmed his support of Lamarckian theory, in *Moses and Monotheism*, the year was 1939, and Freud only had a short time to live. To take back his theory of the inherited qualities of guilt and emotional ambivalence would mean having to rethink the very foundations of psychoanalysis, which might be too much to ask of someone preparing to die.

Freud's interpretation of religion, in many ways, rises or falls with the theory of inherited characteristics. What is important to keep in mind, for the purposes of this study, is that Freud believed he had pinpointed the origin of religion, that it could be "found in the ambivalent relations of son to father, or, to speak psychoanalytically, in *the operation of the Oedipus Complex*." In religion, therefore,

> the son's dependence on the dominant male, and the ambivalence of this filial relation, oscillating between love and hate, and which was first encountered within the primal horde, is projected anew onto the idealized object of religious worship, the father-god. Submission to this object is the first characteristic of belief and it is this above all else which binds believers into a community of faith.[51]

def. of illusion

Freud, of course, was comparing the psyche of the human—that is, male—individual to the collective psyche of, in *Totem and Taboo*, primitive peoples, and, in *Moses and Monotheism*, a single race of people, namely, the Jews. Sandwiched between these two phylogenetic studies, written in 1913 and 1939, respectively, is his most important and famous work on the psychology of religion, *The Future of an Illusion*, which marks a return to the study of ontogenetics and to the origin of religious faith in the life of the individual. Published in 1927, *The Future of an Illusion* is Freud's attempt to determine, once and for all, if there will ever come a day when human individuals can live without the "illusion" of a God in heaven who consoles and protects. An illusion, it must be remembered, "is not the same thing as an error," but is rather a belief motivated by a powerful wish-fulfillment, without any regard for its relation to reality.[52] When human individuals reach adulthood, only to make the unsettling discovery that the feeling of helplessness does not automatically disappear with the passing of childhood, they begin to long for that simpler time and place, when they were under the perpetual care of their parents.

Much of this longing for something or someone more powerful stems from yet another unsettling discovery: there is now, in adulthood, far more to worry about than the mere threat or reality of castration. Adults, whether they like it or not, must now come to terms with the deadly forces of nature, with other human beings and institutions more powerful than themselves, with the ever-present threat of death, and with the instinctual forces of id that never rest until they find expression. Consequently, in the face of such powerful and adversarial forces, one longs again for consolation and protection, only this time consolation and protection must come from something or someone more powerful than an earthly parent. Thus, the image of a benevolent and omnipotent Providence develops in the psyche of human individuals, a divine Providence who will not force us to become the playthings of the mighty and pitiless forces of nature.

While human beings create for themselves, psychically, a benevolent Providence to watch over the world, they still can sense that the world remains a rather dangerous place. Quite frankly, each of us, at one time or another, becomes the plaything of adversarial forces, whether natural or human. Furthermore, we can never be completely happy and fulfilled in this life, for human civilization, of which we are a part, demands from each of us the renunciation of our most basic and primary instinctual pleasures. Freud, while acknowledging that a certain amount of instinctual renunciation is a prerequisite to the establishment and development of any human society, was nonetheless concerned, as we see in *Civilization and Its Discontents,* that the renunciatory demands of human civilization had become *too* demanding. To put this in the form of a question, Is the modern individual sacrificing too much instinctual pleasure, a percentage that the situation at the dawn of human civilization necessitated, but now, in the modern period of human history, seems excessive if not extreme?

This was one of the key topics for discussion at the Frankfurt School for Social Research, and later, in the United States, at the New School of Social Research. What happens, scholars at the Frankfurt School and at the New School wanted to know, when human civilization no longer requires, for purposes of continuity and longevity, such extreme measures of instinctual renunciation? Might there not be a surplus of instinctual renunciation, or, in the words of Herbert Marcuse, a surplus of repression? Certainly, Nazi Germany was a case in point, for anytime the discontents of civilization become unbearable, when the freedom of the individual is sacrificed, in toto, on the altar of national collectivity, an outpouring of unbridled emotion can be expected. Marcuse points out that what we can learn from Freud is that the modern individual, German or not, is living in precarious times: "The more civilization progresses, the more powerful its apparatus for the development and gratification of social needs becomes, the more oppressive are the sacrifices that it has to impose on individuals in order to maintain the necessary instinctual structure."[53]

All of this suggests a very painful and unsatisfying state of existence, which necessitates, even further, the need and wish for a benevolent Providence, someone bigger and more powerful than human life. And yet, does the illusion of a divine Providence ameliorate, to any appreciable extent, the human condition? Freud, as we might expect, had his doubts: "In every age," he wrote with extraordinary candor, "immorality has found no less support in religion than morality has," so that "if the achievements of religion in respect to man's happiness, susceptibility to culture and moral control are no better than this, the question cannot but arise whether we are not overrating its necessity for mankind, and whether we do wisely in basing our cultural demands upon it."[54] As pure and pristine as we would like it to be, religion, according to Freud, is primarily in the service of human civilization. It functions to reinforce the demands of culture, otherwise known as the status quo.

The human individual, by embracing the "universal neurosis" called "religion," settles for an arrested state of intellectual and emotional development. Freud laments that "the whole thing is so patently infantile, so foreign to reality, that to anyone with a friendly attitude to humanity it is painful to think that the great majority of mortals will never be able to rise above this view of life."[55] At this point, we can detect hints of Ludwig Feuerbach, who likewise harbored a "friendly attitude to humanity," calling on human beings to claim their own intellectual power and to stop emptying themselves into the heavens. What, then, is the alternative, if religion is no longer the cornerstone of human civilization? For Freud, a product of the latter days of the Enlightenment, the answer can be summed up in a word: *science*. Only when we begin educating ourselves and our children and their children to reality, instead of the illusion of providential care and protection, will we have the courage to face, with an attitude of benign acceptance and resignation, reality *as it is* rather than reality *as it should be*. This scientific age of reason will stem the intellectual retardation of the human race, caused by our irrational overdependence on, and devotion to, a benevolent Providence.

Freud's psychology of religion, it bears emphasizing, is focused on the *masculine* reactivation of the Oedipus Complex, both ontogenetically and phylogenetically. The origin of religion, as Freud saw it, can be found in the ambivalent relation—oscillating between love and hate—of son to father, in one's own childhood as well as the primordial beginnings of the human race. At crisis moments, the male individual, feeling rather helpless, can reactivate the memory of his own father and that of the father of the primal horde, as a means of coping with the anxiety of human living. This memory, or the "return of the repressed," is then, as Michael Palmer has observed, projected anew onto the idealized object of religious worship and devotion, onto God the Father Almighty. Submission to the idealized object recapitulates the early days of childhood—both the boy's and that of the human race—when the boy lived in fear of a more powerful father, but was nevertheless assured of the father's protection. The actual killing of the primal father, and the fantasized killing of the father of childhood, have created a unique sense of guilt in the male psyche.

What this means, in very practical terms, is that the masculine superego is more highly developed than the feminine superego, owing its enlargement to the identification with the powerful father. And since, as Freud put it, the superego "contains the germ from which all religions have evolved," one may rightly deduce that the male will lead the way when it comes to the matter of religious faith. As Van Herik will point out in chapter 4, Freud was merely describing the present state of *normal* masculinity, for to proceed to the loftier and more noble state of *ideal* masculinity will require the undiluted exchange of religious faith for reason and science. For the time being, as human beings make their way through the religious stage of evolution, Freud reminds us that "the male sex seems to have taken the lead in . . . moral acquisitions; and they seem to have been transmitted to women by cross-inheritance."[56] Freud, who was perfectly candid when he wanted to be, was also, at other times, rather disingenuous. From all he has said about religion and gender, we know only too well where he really stands: the male sex not only *seems* to have taken the lead in moral and religious acquisitions; it *has* taken the lead, just as it will take the lead in scientific acquisitions during the next stage of human evolution.

As I conclude this chapter on Freud's interpretation of religion, I want to set the stage for what comes next, methodologically, namely, the critical-analysis portion of the book. The work of the three theorists, Ricoeur, Rizzuto, and Van Herik, will form the foundation of the critical appraisal of Freud and his theory. For now, it is enough to state the obvious: there is much in Freud's interpretation of religion that not only invites but also demands evaluation and a critical response from the religious believer. To be sure, the Freudian themes that invite critical reflection are myriad. For example, in terms of his phylogenetic reconstruction of human history, Freud's anthropological and historical evidence is, to put it mildly, rather dubious. The theory of an original primal horde, dominated by a single male leader, was derived from Darwin's *speculative* hypothesis, which Freud took to be the gospel truth.

Freud, seemingly the quintessential champion of the scientific method, regularly criticized the believer for hiding his or her religious faith behind the cloak of unfalsifiability. And while it is certainly true that believers do at times hide their religious faith behind a cloak of unfalsifiability, Freud himself seems to have been guilty of the very same thing, of failing to distance himself completely from unfalsifiable speculations. Specifically, how can we ever know for sure if there really was an original primal horde, an original father-son ambivalence, an original patricide, and an original sense of guilt, the effects of which are still keenly felt by every young boy? It is one thing to say that you can draw a straight line from an adult's present-day image of God directly back to his or her object relations during childhood, but it is another thing to say that you can extend that line of origination back before the individual even came into existence, back into the murky primordial beginnings of the human race. Freud's data, at this point, were unfalsifiable, whether he cared to admit it or not.

For the purposes of this study, I will limit the critical analysis to the Freudian themes that have direct bearing on the idea of religious faith as psychological projection. For example, Ricoeur, as we will see in chapter 2, believes that Freud's theory of the psychical reactivation of the oedipal father, and its projection onto the idealized object of religious worship, the father-god, captures the essence of an individual's religious faith anytime the individual passively tolerates the moral condemnation of God in exchange for God's eternal protection and consolation. Is there not, Ricoeur will ask, a healthier and more meaningful alternative? Not within a Freudian framework, for a more meaningful alternative would have to come from the psychical realm of creativity and imagination, which Freud, from the get-go, devalues as a lesser reality or even as unreality. Do human beings, then, Ricoeur wants to know, *need* their creative illusions and visions and dreams, in order to rise above a fatalistic resignation to material reality?

When Freud speaks of the "education to reality," he means, quite literally, the education to external material reality, which for him is the "really real." Psychical reality, on the other hand, to the extent it can be called "reality" at all, is always an illusory reality, an illusory realm in which neurotics and religious believers find temporary escape from the harshness of the real external world. Rizzuto, who completely agrees with Freud's basic premise, that the origin of an individual's God-image can be traced directly back to his or her object relations during early childhood, will still take Freud to task for his devaluation of psychical space. As we will see in chapter 3, she will pose various questions, including the following: Is the psychological projection of one's earliest object relations always an immature or neurotic defensive maneuver? Can there ever be, in the context of religious faith, a healthy projection of our early object relations? And, is the longing for consolation, in the face of life's dangers and disappointments, always, in every time and place, an expression of psychological immaturity and/or neurosis? Can there ever be a healthy regression, not only to the oceanic feeling of eternal oneness with the mother, but even to the psychical images and representations of the oedipal father?

These questions about Freud and his theory beg a more basic question, one that Van Herik will address in chapter 4: Is there a connection between the devaluation of the psyche of believers and the devaluation of the psychical world of women? Freud's theory, she will argue, gives us some important clues about present-day attitudes toward both religion and gender. For example, if we as a culture devalue, even subtly, the efficacy of religious faith, approaching it with an attitude of superficial regard, are we not, Van Herik will want to know, also devaluing the emotional life of women? Or, to reverse the equation, if we undervalue the emotional life of women, are we not also undervaluing the spiritual life of both men and women? These are some of the questions to keep in mind as we work our way through the following chapters of critical analysis.

■ T W O ■

What Freud Can and Cannot Teach
the Religious Believer

It is, in fact, one of the most important tasks of psychic hygiene to pay continual attention to the symptomatology of unconscious contents and processes, for the good reason that the conscious mind is always in danger of becoming one-sided, of keeping to well-worn paths and getting stuck in blind alleys.

C. G. Jung, *Aion*

I t is Paul Ricoeur, more than any other scholar, who has stirred my interest in Freud. Specifically, what stands out for me, more than anything else, is Ricoeur's bold and definitive statement, in the very last paragraph of his impressive work, *Freud and Philosophy*: the religious believer owes Freud a "no" *and* a "yes." As I pointed out in the introduction, it was this statement from Ricoeur that raised the ire of several of my seminary students. The last thing these seminarians wanted to do, as they fine-tuned their theology in preparation for ordained ministry, was to entertain the possibility that Freud may actually have something important and relevant to say about their religious faith.

Nor are seminarians the only ones who have difficulty giving Freud a definitive "yes." Frederick Crews, the writer and professor emeritus of English at the University of California, Berkeley, has also taken exception to Ricoeur's suggestion, albeit for different reasons. Crews, in the introduction of his book, *Unauthorized Freud*, lets us know, in no uncertain terms, that he has problems with Ricoeur's hermeneutical approach to Freud: psychoanalysis, for Ricoeur, "is not a science but a hermeneutic (interpretive) activity, in which case it should be judged only on intuitive and empathic, not empirical grounds." However, because Freud "repeatedly and emphatically declared his brainchild to be a science," his "meaning claims," according to Crews, are tied to causal assumptions that cannot "be set aside without disemboweling the entire system."[1]

Fair enough, but then where does that leave us? It would seem that we are back to where we started from, in the all-too-familiar context of an either-or conceptual framework. Crews's inflexibility, on the matter of a hermeneutical approach to Freud, does not seem all that different from the inflexibility of my indignant student in the seminary classroom. In this particular framework, the student of Freud, not to mention the religious believer, is left having to make a choice between one of two extremes: either embrace the totality of Freudian theory, or reject it completely. For Crews and for many religious believers, the only option is the latter. "The fact," writes Crews, "that Freudian beliefs are underwritten by nothing but interpretations is doubtless awkward, but efforts to turn that deficiency to argumentative advantage are doomed to be unavailing."[2]

But does Crews's wholesale dismissal of Freudian theory and a hermeneutical approach to Freud get us anywhere new? Not if our goal is finding a way to creatively live *within* the dialectical tension of opposing views. Crews's approach to Freud leaves us with an either-or framework, which, unfortunately, takes us back to square one and to the reality of a hopeless impasse. While this is not a book on Frederick Crews, the vigorous challenge that he issues to Freudian theory and to Ricoeur's hermeneutical approach to Freud must nevertheless be taken very seriously. That said, believers will have to look to someone other than Crews, if they intend to find a way to live *within* the dialectical tension between their religious faith and Freud's interpretation of religion. That someone is Ricoeur.

Ricoeur, for starters, refuses to deal with Freud and psychoanalysis in absolutist terms, either positive or negative. Like Sandra Schneiders, he champions the hermeneutical method, which for him means working within the fundamental energic tension between two opposing poles: "At one pole is a hermeneutics of belief, which aims to restore the meaning of a text, allowing its authentic message to manifest itself anew," while "at the other pole is a hermeneutics of suspicion, which reduces and demystifies, relentlessly stripping away the illusions and idols that we take for reality."[3] Thus, while religious believers may initially find themselves drawn to the either-or approach of Crews, because of his unrelenting critique of Freudian theory, they would do well to consider Ricoeur's more balanced hermeneutical approach to Freud. As we learned earlier, Ricoeur reminds us that Freud has done nothing short of introducing a uniquely influential interpretation of the phenomenon of culture and of religion as a fundamental component of culture. Whether Freud's meaning claims are tied to erroneous causal assumptions or not, we must still come to terms with the fact that we as a culture analyze ourselves through Freud, a fact of *extreme importance* that must be understood and evaluated. It is to Ricoeur's evaluation of Freudian theory that we now turn our attention. In the process, we will discover that the less we know of Freud the less we will know about ourselves as individuals and as a culture.

■ THE "TEXT" OF CONSCIOUSNESS ■

I disagree with Crews's view, that because Freud tied his meaning claims about psychoanalysis to certain scientific assumptions we are therefore obligated to limit our engagement with him to the field of science. Ricoeur, for one, is convinced that we can engage Freud and his theory hermeneutically, if we keep in mind the fundamental meaning and nature of hermeneutics. "By hermeneutics," Ricoeur explains, "we shall understand the theory of the rules that preside over an exegesis—that is, over the interpretation of a particular text, or of a group of signs that may be viewed as a text . . . and by the extension of the concept of exegesis to all signs bearing an analogy to a text."[4] If we accept Ricoeur's definition of hermeneutics, then psychoanalysis can in fact be evaluated, not only scientifically, but also hermeneutically.

By keeping in mind the last portion of Ricoeur's definition, we see that the concept of exegesis, which is usually applied philologically to the interpretation of a written text, can, *by extension,* be applied to any and all signs bearing an analogy to a written text. Texts to be interpreted, then, might be, as we would expect, a literary work, a scriptural passage, or a theological treatise, or, maybe unexpectedly, certain phenomena we encounter in the field of psychoanalysis: a dream, hysteria, the unconscious, or even consciousness. The discipline of hermeneutics, by nature, is primarily a means of getting at the deeper meaning hidden beneath the more obvious surface content of a text. For example, with a written text, we want to know what the author was thinking when he or she wrote it, what the author was hoping to evoke in the mind of the reader, and if the text means the same thing to today's reader as it did to its initial audience of readers, all of which takes the investigation beyond surface inquiry.

Now, if we juxtapose the discipline of hermeneutics with that of psychoanalysis, we begin to see that it is not that much of a stretch to say that Freud's modus operandi was, in a certain sense, hermeneutical, in that he, too, was looking for the deeper meaning behind the surface content of various "texts." Crews is exactly right when he says that Freud never envisioned psychoanalysis as a form of hermeneutics, and may have actually loathed the association, if he were still living today. Nevertheless, if our goal is to fully understand the Western individual and his or her religious faith, then the hermeneutical application of psychoanalysis to the individual's psychological and spiritual development can only broaden and enrich our study.

For Ricoeur, the hermeneutical method, as noted, is defined by the juxtaposition of two opposing poles. At one pole is a hermeneutics of belief and meaning, to be held firmly in dialectical tension with the other pole, a hermeneutics of suspicion that reduces and demystifies, stripping away the illusions and idols we take for reality. According to Ricoeur, the quintessential hermeneutics of suspicion vis-à-vis the human individual, in general, and the religious believer, in particular, comes to us from Freud and from the discipline of psychoanalysis. There have been, Ricoeur admits, other "masters" of suspicion—for instance, Karl Marx and Friedrich Nietzsche—but it is Freud who stands above all others as *the* master of suspicion. Why Freud? It is mainly because Freud, more than anyone else, has delivered the "blow" of psychological humiliation to humanity's universal narcissism.

To begin with, Copernicus dealt the human race a cosmological humiliation, when his research revealed that earth, and, by association, human beings are not the center of the universe. This was followed by a biological humiliation delivered courtesy of Charles Darwin, the finding that we are in fact directly related to the rest of the animal world. But Freud, as Ricoeur wants us to see, pushed the matter of humiliation even further, when he demonstrated, through the application of psychoanalysis, that human individuals are not even the rulers of their own psyche. Ricoeur puts it this way:

> Narcissism opposed the acceptance of the discoveries of Copernicus, for they stripped us of the illusion of being at the center of the universe; it opposed Darwin's evolutionist theories, which plunge us into the vast flux of life; finally it resists psychoanalysis because the latter shakes the primacy and sovereignty of consciousness. A new aspect of the conflict between the pleasure principle and the reality principle is brought to light: narcissism interposes itself between ourselves and reality: that is why the truth is always wounding to our narcissism.[5]

Much of the resistance, according to Freud, stems from our overconfidence in immediate consciousness. We could say, with a fair amount of certainty, that the whole history of psychoanalysis has been largely an exercise of suspicion aimed at the "text" of immediate consciousness and subjectivity. Freudian topography—consciousness, preconsciousness, and unconsciousness—teaches us, first and foremost, that "the most archaic significations are organized in a 'place' of meaning that is separate from the place where immediate consciousness reigns."[6] And if that were not enough, "consciousness is cut off from its own sense by an impediment it can neither direct nor know: . . . the dynamism of repression," which, Ricoeur believes, "is the key to Freudian topography."[7] It is also the key to understanding what makes us so resistant to the idea that we are not the center of the universe, that we are fundamentally related to the animal world, that, after Freud, we are not even the ruler of our own interiority.

As a species, we have gotten used to Copernicus' cosmological humiliation, and we have even, for the most part, gotten used to Darwin's biological humiliation, even though there are still pockets of resistance. In accepting the findings of Copernicus and Darwin, we have, to be sure, given up much, which may explain our reluctance to be open-minded about the findings of psychoanalysis. Indeed, if we accept Freud's conclusions, if we concede that the most significant meanings are not on a conscious level, but rather in a place or region separate and far removed from immediate consciousness, what then? Will there be anything left in which we can take pride as a species, anything that makes us feel special and unique? Furthermore, how can the Christian believer reconcile this finding of Freud with the theology of *Imago Dei*, the fact that human beings, as we read in the first chapter of Genesis, have been created in the very image of God?

Ricoeur is unfazed: the only way the religious believer can ignore the seminal and indisputable finding of Freud is through the dynamism of repression and resistance. To put this in Freudian terms, we could say that the individual who refuses to acknowledge the humbling of immediate consciousness "is destined to remain a child forever."[8] Ricoeur's message is essentially Socratic, in that he believes that an unexamined life is not worth living. Taking the Socratic precept one step further, it is not difficult to imagine Ricoeur saying to the religious believer, "an unexamined and unreflective religious faith, a faith that refuses to integrate even the more substantiated findings of Freud, is not worth having." Since we as a culture have internalized so much Freudian theory, and tend to analyze ourselves through its interpretative lens, we cannot sidestep psychoanalysis and then assume that we are in possession of a religious faith capable of meeting the demands of a postmodern age.

What Freud has taught us is that the human individual's self-reflection is hardly an original act. Hence, after Freud, it is virtually impossible to believe that we enjoy immediate self-possession or perfect self-identity. Any attestation of self-determination, personal immediacy, and religious selfhood must, in Ricoeur's own words, be "inseparable from an exercise of suspicion."[9] After Freud has systematically applied his hermeneutics of suspicion to the text of the human psyche, we can only talk of the dispossession of consciousness. Consciousness, therefore, which to many philosophers, poets and theologians, down through the centuries, has been "proof" of the loftiness of the human mind, would now seem, after Freud, to be humiliated beyond repair. Ricoeur, however, is quick to point out that what has been humiliated is the *pretension* of consciousness, and not consciousness itself.

Ricoeur wants us to see that consciousness, after it has been critiqued by Freud, has become a task, a *Bewusstwerden* or "becoming-consciousness," rather than a *Bewusstsein*, that is, a "static given" or "being-consciousness." The individual's subjectivity, to a very large extent, is fictitious and is real "only insofar as it is placed in suspense, unrealized [and] potentialized."[10] This, of course, is a radical departure from a Cartesian worshipfulness of consciousness, which, during the modern period, has had such an enormous and influential impact on Christian theology. The Cartesian stance—recall René Descartes' famous, "I think, therefore I am"—is a reflection of a *Bewusstsein*, and therefore stands, after Freud, in need of immediate reassessment.

Descartes' revolutionary statement would be more relevant if it were reflective of a *Bewusstwerden*: "I think, therefore I am becoming," would seem to more aptly capture the essence of the human psyche. Moreover, long before Descartes had his revolutionary and cognitive breakthrough, before he had consciously and willingly posited himself, he had already, like the rest of us, "been placed in being at the instinctual level."[11] Freud, then, much like Aristotle, Spinoza, Leibniz, and Hegel, situates desire, rather than cognition, at the center of human existence, and forces us to ask ourselves a very basic and fundamental question: "Is what we say and do a reflection of what we desire?"[12]

To put all of this in the context of religious faith, we could reword the question, asking the religious believer, "Is what you confess and believe a reflection of what you truly desire?" Or is there an internal disconnect between the person's conscious profession of faith and his or her unconscious desire? For example, a believer who is asked to comment on his or her attachment to religious faith, may say that it is a natural response to the greatness and goodness of God. So far so good. However, if we were to give the believer a gentle nudge, inviting the person to be more disclosive, what we might discover is that while the believer cognitively connects God's greatness and goodness with a personal profession of faith, emotionally, there are other reasons for believing. These "emotional truths" might include the

religion fam = order structu protcht [handwritten annotation]

fact that religious faith brings order and structure to an otherwise chaotic world; it assures me that human beings are not, after all, alone in the universe; religious faith affirms that even though we will die, a part of us goes on living; and, as long as we worship God, we will always be in God's favor.

In terms of getting at these deeper emotional truths, Ricoeur believes that psychoanalysis, more than anything else, has the capacity to take us back to our unconscious roots and to the instinctual level of our existence through what Maurice Merleau-Ponty called the "archaeology of the subject."[13] This is the archaism of instinct, "the anteriority of the ontic plane to the reflective plane, the priority of *I am* to *I think*."[14] And what, we may ask, does the archaeology of the subject reveal, particularly the archaeology of the religious believer? What is immediately apparent is that individuals are oftentimes overconfident in their conscious, taken-for-granted reality and in their abstractly encased beliefs, values, and standards. Freud's hermeneutics of suspicion, then, "has the value of being a protest against the abstract nature of the theory of knowledge and its alleged purity; this reduction of the act of knowing as such attests to the nonautonomy of knowledge, and its rootedness in existence."[15]

As we can see, Ricoeur firmly believes that we can learn much from the "schooling" of Freud, as we apply his theory phenomenologically to various "texts." We have already highlighted the text of consciousness, and discovered that there can be powerful contradictions in our psychical life "between conscious intention and unconscious desire and being and that in any case what we believe ourselves to be doing is in no way identical with what is in fact transpiring in our human being."[16] This is precisely why Freud conceived of psychoanalytic treatment as that which attempts to make the patient's unconscious desire and truth more conscious. The fact that we have to make our unconscious desire conscious underscores the fundamental dualism that is at the heart of Western civilization. From Plato to the apostle Paul to Descartes, we can trace the dualistic thread that gives precedence to soul over body, to spirit over flesh, and to mind over matter. All of us living in the Western world have been taught, to some extent, to distance ourselves from our unconscious desires and instincts, or, in theological terms, the *flesh*. Christian theology has often taken this a step further, admonishing believers to triumph, rather emphatically, over their desires and emotions.

Religious believers, within this framework, can only become fragmented individuals, since little or no emphasis is placed upon wholeness and integration. Our unconscious desires, however, as Freud has taught us, cannot stay underground forever, but are destined to resurface again and again, sometimes explosively and destructively. For example, in my clinical practice, I sometimes work with individuals who seem to have been blindsided by the sudden reemergence of certain unconscious desires. Clients inform me that they honestly believed they had, through the grace and power of God, triumphed over their addictions to alcohol, sex, rage and so forth, only to find themselves overcome yet again by such powerful internal forces. Had their conscious intention and unconscious desire been better integrated within themselves, they might have been less surprised by, in Freudian terms, the *return of the repressed*. Furthermore, if conscious intention and unconscious desire were more integrated, within self and psyche, these individuals would have a greater degree of personal power and agency, to act upon their desires if they so choose, rather than having the desires repeatedly act upon them in painful ways.

■ THE "TEXT" OF RELIGIOUS FAITH ■

There are, according to Ricoeur, other "texts" besides consciousness to which a Freudian hermeneutics of suspicion can be effectively applied. He highlights various texts of culture, including art, music, science and, especially for the believer, the text of religion and theology. In fact, when it comes to the text of religious faith, Ricoeur is unwavering: the religious believer, living in the Western world, stands in urgent need of Freud's interrogative "schooling." If the believer's religious faith, following an intensive encounter with Freud, fails the test of authenticity, then it was hardly a faith adequate in meeting the demands and challenges of the postmodern age. Or so it would seem. Religious believers—whether they be seminarians, clergy, theologians, or laity—may very well point out that it ought to be the other way around: the religious community should be using a hermeneutics of suspicion on the "text" of Freud, in order to get the whole story behind his overt devaluation of the religious life.

There is, to be sure, plenty of justification for probing the depths of the Freudian text. For example, it is not too difficult to see that certain powerful and formative events had a lasting impact upon Freud, and left an indelible impression in the depths of his psyche. As a young boy, Freud was deeply troubled by his father's humiliation at the hands of certain Christian townspeople; his father, a Jew, had had his hat knocked off his head. And certainly, the horrors of the First World War, with the death and carnage and destruction practically on his front doorstep, could only prejudice Freud's view of human nature, could only lead him to further doubt the existence of a benevolent Providence. Little wonder, then, that Freud would theorize the existence of a cosmic battle between life and death, between Eros and Thanatos, a universal struggle for the heart of the human race. Little wonder that he sounds so sarcastic, when he writes, "And it is this battle of the giants that our nurse-maids try to appease with their lullaby about Heaven."[17]

Religious believers, in turning the tables on Freud, and critiquing the "text" of his life and theory, may also point out that Freud offers us little in the way of prescription. Said another way, while he has much to say, *descriptively*, about the tragic human condition, he has far less, if anything to say about the amelioration of our flawed condition. Ricoeur sees this coming, and responds to the believer's turn-the-tables strategy with these words:

> This is why I think psychoanalysis has nothing specific to say for or against . . . prescriptive or normative thought. I know it is willing to remain silent on this point. Its function is to pose prior questions: Are our wishes free or constrained? Regain the ability to speak and to enjoy, and all the rest will be given to you as a bonus. Is this not to say, along with Augustine, "Love, and do what you want?" For if your love has rediscovered its place [*sa justesse*], your will will also find its justice—but by grace rather than by law.[18]

Keeping in mind the earlier discussion of the text of human consciousness, we can proceed to paraphrase Ricoeur. For example, the function of psychoanalysis is to pose such questions as the following: Is what we say and do a reflection of what we unconsciously desire? Is what we consciously believe about ourselves in any way identical with what is in fact transpiring at the core of our being? If we cannot answer these questions at least partially in the affirmative, then we cannot say, with Augustine, "Love, and do what you want." But how can we ever be in touch with what we truly want and desire, if we steadfastly refuse to entertain any of these "prior questions?" Without hermeneutics of suspicion, religious believers will find it especially difficult to integrate, psychically and spiritually, certain conscious beliefs with unconscious desires. In practical terms, this means that they will have difficulty accessing the emotional and spiritual depths of personal experience. In biblical terms, it means that the way to abundant living is foreclosed.

For Ricoeur, one of the fundamental "prior questions" has to do with the distinction between the objective and the subjective aspects of religious faith. Put in the form of a question, How much of a believer's religious faith is about a transcendent and benevolent Providence and how much of it is about the particular individual and his or her longing to be consoled and protected? Religious faith, according to Ricoeur, will always bear, to some extent, residual traces of "primitive immaturity."[19] Every religious believer, Ricoeur wants us to remember, from the most brilliant and sophisticated theologian to the average layperson, who knows and probably cares very little about the complexities and intricacies of religion, is the bearer of this primitive immaturity. It is, therefore, a matter of degree, and certainly not of kind.

If I take myself as an object lesson, and self-reflectively apply a Freudian hermeneutics of suspicion to the "text" of my own faith and psyche, I have no choice but to admit that Ricoeur, with the help of Freud, has identified a fundamental aspect of the need for religion. Indeed, even though I am an ordained Presbyterian minister, a professionally certified pastoral counselor, and a teacher of psychology and theology—that is, I ought to possess some religious and theological sophistication—I must confess that when I am in the midst of a crisis situation, an ineffable longing and yearning for something or someone to make things better and right is inevitably and instinctively reactivated, something that Ricoeur would surely label as *primitive immaturity*. Freud would call this the "return of the repressed" oedipal father within me, and while the benevolent Providence I had in mind during certain crisis situations did have a number of masculine features, this was not the case during other crisis situations. At other crisis moments, a more maternal God came to mind, in response to my ineffable longing. In any case, I suspect that I am not the only one to have experienced this archetypal reactivation of the primitive longing for a consoling presence.

Quite frankly, it was after I applied, nondefensively, the Freudian hermeneutics of suspicion to the "text" of self and faith that I really began to understand what an effective teacher Freud can be. True, I had already come to the conclusion that Freud was not, contrary to the opinion of many religious believers, entirely wrong about the nature of religious faith. Yet his ultimate conclusion about the need for religion, that it is a means of helping human beings cope with their feelings of helplessness and powerlessness in the face of more powerful external and internal forces, seemed to me, at the time, brash if not offensive. And now, as I look back on various crisis moments—for instance, being laid off from a position in business and industry; being turned down for a parish position, even after the search committee had offered to call me; being stranded in the middle of nowhere, in the broiling heat of the Atacama Desert in Chile; suffering through a debilitating illness;

purpose of rel. according to Freud

and trying to pay bills, when there was little or no money—I can admit that my prayers to God, at those times, were not simply an attempt to get myself centered and focused on the resources already at my disposal. These prayers were also a rather primitive plea to God for divine intervention and immediate relief.

The fundamental purpose of religion, Freud had argued, is to make human living more bearable and human suffering more understandable. Said another way, religion is the art of bearing the hardships of life, or the "discontents" of a civilization that forces each and everyone of us to renounce our most basic and primary instinctual pleasures, so that we may instead submit ourselves to the greater collective good, to the cultural evolution of the species. My religious faith, I humbly discovered, after I had exposed it to the Freudian hermeneutics of suspicion, was indeed the bearer of residual traces of primitive immaturity, of some primitive and ineffable longing for consolation in the face of life's hardships and discontents.

But religion, according to Freud, is more than a matter of longing for consolation and solace. It is also, as we learned in chapter 1, a matter of longing for protection against the powerful and impassive forces of nature, against more powerful human beings and even against ourselves, or the part of ourselves that does make cowards of us all: our accusatory conscience or superego. The human individual is a being threatened both by the forces from without, *like* any other animal, and by the forces from within, *unlike* any other animal. For Freud, the former—the external forces from without—are considerably easier to defend against. Civilization, through various means— science, technology, medicine, education, and law enforcement—does a fairly good job of protecting us against potentially harmful and malevolent natural and human forces. This is the return or the dividend we receive, all because we have renounced our most basic instinctual pleasures.

The civilizational struggle against the dangerous forces of nature, however, is never entirely successful. Human beings finally reach adulthood only to discover that they are still the poor naked wretches that bide the pelting of this pitiless storm. Nor are adults simply pelted by the same storms they weathered as children. The storms have suddenly intensified, exponentially. We nervously and sometimes reluctantly drop our children off at school, after having read about the latest incident of school violence in the morning newspaper; we face the perpetual threat of natural disasters, which could conceivably turn our lives upside down in a fraction of a second; today could be the day when our health takes a turn for the worse (Fiorella Domenico's predicament, as we will see in the next chapter), or when we experience the effects of financial misfortune; and, last but certainly not least, today could be the day when our airplane experiences mechanical difficulties.

In many ways, our adult helplessness, though sometimes intense and formidable, is simply a continuation and a repetition of the helplessness we experienced as children. This is what led Freud to the rather bold conclusion, in *The Future of an Illusion* (1927), that the human individual is destined to remain a child forever. Ricoeur would agree, in the sense that human beings and their various expressions of religious faith will invariably manifest, to some extent, residual traces of primitive immaturity. The logical question, then, is what keeps human beings from giving free reign to their most basic biological desires, since civilization is never entirely successful at protecting them against the deadly forces of nature? Indeed, it seems as if we sacrifice so much of our individuality and instinctuality on the altar of collectivity, only to end up getting a rather modest amount of protection and satisfaction in return.

At this point, civilization, in order to keep the individual's level of frustration at a minimum, falls back upon a reserve strategy, namely, what Freud referred to as an "illusion." Recall that for Freud an illusion is not the same thing as an error, but is rather a belief motivated by wish fulfillment, without any regard for its relation to external reality. What we wish for, as human beings, is something bigger and more powerful than civilization, something or someone to guarantee us eternal protection against the pitiless forces of nature. Thus, we never completely outgrow the helplessness of childhood, both our own and that of the species. This could obviously lead us to despair or anarchic revolt, if it were not for the fact that civilization creates for us the *illusion* of an exalted benevolent Provider and Protector. "The question Freud poses," writes Ricoeur, "is not that of God as such but that of the god of men and his economic function in the balance sheet of the instinctual renunciations, substitutive satisfactions, and compensations by which men try to make life tolerable." Ricoeur continues:

> The key to illusion is the harshness of life, which is barely tolerable for man, since he not only understands and feels pain but yearns for consolation as a result of his innate narcissism. As we have seen, culture's task is not only to reduce human desire but also to defend man against the crushing superiority of nature. Illusion is the reserve method used by culture when the effective struggle against the evils of existence either has not begun or has not yet succeeded, or has failed, whether temporarily or definitively.

duty & conscience

It creates gods to exorcise fear, to reconcile man to the cruelty of his lot, and to compensate for the suffering of culture.[20]

Illusion, so it would seem, is culture's fail-safe method, something that will hopefully satisfy the individual, particularly the religious believer, when all else fails. This is all well and good, as long as we are talking about external forces, or the forces *outside* the human psyche. But what about the forces *inside* the human psyche, the internal and instinctual forces of id? Here is where even the reserve method of illusion begins breaking down, necessitating, by way of certain representatives of culture—parents, teachers, peers, and tradition—the instillation of an internal force and censor. What is being described is the agency of conscience, or, to put it in the context of Freud's later topography of the human psyche—id, ego, and superego—the agency of the superego. It was Freud who, in his own as well as Ricoeur's estimation, delivered the blow of psychological humiliation to humanity's universal narcissism, teaching us with his schooling that, contrary to conventional wisdom and Cartesian epistemology, we are not even the ruler of our own interior world. This finding, as the history of psychoanalysis plainly reveals, overtly applies to the psyche of the neurotic individual. It also, Ricoeur wants us to know, applies to the psyche of the religious believer, particularly the believer who regards faith and spirituality as little more than the means to the end of moral uprightness.

Ricoeur, at this point, issues something of a warning to the religious believer, something that the schooling of Freud makes abundantly clear: there is such a thing as a pathology of duty and conscience. In other words, while we must guard against a pathology of desire and instinct, we must also guard against falling prey to the "illusion" that this can simply be accomplished by means of a reverse pathology of duty and conscience. For example, when a religious leader "falls from grace," after the disclosure of, say, financial or sexual misconduct, there is often a tendency on the part of the other members of the religious community to clamp down on their own personal desires and emotions, out of fear that they may follow suit and lose control of their own instinctual appetites. But this, according to Ricoeur, is hardly a creative and healthy response to the leader's pathology of desire. Certainly, after Freud, religious believers cannot simply point the finger at the sinner's overt pathology of desire, without first facing the pathology of their own rigid morality.

After Freud, religious believers cannot merely think in terms of a pathology of desire and instinct. A pathology of duty, conscience and morality, the manifestation of a harsh and repressive superego, is every bit as deadly. Ricoeur illustrates this particular point when he links the dynamics of guilt with the dynamics of scrupulosity: "With guilt," he observes, "there arises indeed a sort of demand which can be called *scrupulosity* and whose ambiguous character is extremely interesting." Freud, no doubt, would find the ambiguous character of scrupulosity to be more than "extremely interesting." In fact, he would argue that it is essentially a reflection of unresolved issues that initially surfaced during the oedipal stage of development, rather than proof of one's love for, and devotion to, God. Ricoeur would agree. He continues with his juxtaposition of guilt and scrupulosity, which is worth quoting at length:

> A scrupulous conscience is a delicate consciousness, a precise consciousness, enamored of increasing perfection; it is a consciousness anxious to observe all the commandments, to satisfy the law in all things, without making an exception of any sector of existence, without taking into account exterior obstacles, for example the persecution of a prince, and which gives as much importance to little things as to great. But at the same time scrupulosity marks the entrance of moral consciousness into its own pathology; a scrupulous person encloses himself in the inextricable labyrinth of commandments; obligation takes on an enumerative and cumulative character, which contrasts with the simplicity and sobriety of the commandment to love God and man. The scrupulous consciousness never stops adding new commandments. . . . The scrupulous person never arrives at satisfying all the commandments or even any one. At the same time, even the notion of obedience is perverted; obedience to a commandment, because it is commanded, becomes more important than love of neighbor and even love of God; this exactitude in obedience is what we call legalism.[21]

If our intention is to be completely knowledgeable about the varied layers of human attachment to God and religious faith, we must look, not only to the theological hermeneutics of belief, but also to the psychological hermeneutics of suspicion. Freud, through the application of a psychoanalytic hermeneutics of suspicion, clearly demonstrated that while believers consciously profess their unconditional devotion to God, there are also certain egoistic needs—feeling consoled and protected—that get satisfied at the same time. If, however, these egoistic needs become the driving force of one's faith, then, as Ricoeur points out, the believer is in possession of an unreflective faith of the "first naïveté," a faith that has yet to be subjected to a herme-neutics of suspicion.

Nor is an unreflective faith of the first naïveté limited to those with less theological knowledge and sophistication. Martin Luther, as Erik Erikson has demonstrated, even had difficulty keeping moral scrupulosity separate from religious devotion to God. "In confession, for example," Erikson in-forms us, "[Luther] was so meticulous in the attempt to be truthful that he spelled out every intention as well as every deed; he splintered relatively acceptable purities into smaller and smaller impurities; he reported tempta-tions in historical sequence, starting back in childhood; and after having confessed for hours, would ask for special appointments in order to correct previous statements." Erikson, with subtle humor, then adds; "[Luther's] pre-ceptor threatened to punish him for obstruction of confession."[22] This, of course, was centuries before psychotherapy took hold, otherwise Luther would have been referred to a therapist or counselor to work on personal issues, issues that were, by nature, more psychological than theological.

What we now know, centuries later, thanks largely to Freud and psy-choanalysis, is that a pathology of duty and conscience, manifested in the scrupulous attention one gives to the details and order of one's religious faith, is just as detrimental to one's emotionality and spirituality as a pathology of unleashed desire. Freud, it should also be noted, would have had a field day with the report that Luther could remember, apparently with perfect recall, temptations and sins dating all the way back into the early days of his childhood. Even the mighty reformer, as it were, had certain residual traces of primitive immaturity. Luther's primitive immaturity, as we learn from Erikson's psychobiographical research, harked back to a rather painful rela-tionship with a harsh and demanding father, whose image, in the mind of Luther, could be held in check only through massive repression and pains-taking devotion to God and faith.

The exalted Deity, Freud had argued, not only consoles religious be-lievers, but also gives them the feeling that they are eternally protected against pitiless internal and external forces. But what is required of the believer, in exchange for this eternal protection? The answer, not surpris-ingly, is reminiscent of the expectations of the oedipal father for his child: believers must willingly submit to what the Deity determines to be appropri-ate discipline. Religious believers are offered consolation and protection, but, at the same time, they must accept the Deity's accusations and constraints, presumably for their own good. This, again, as with Luther, resembles the oedipal arrangement of early childhood.

C. G. Jung, in *Answer to Job*, noted that the consolation and protection offered by the Deity were in fact inextricably linked to the dynamic of accusation and punishment. Jung directs our attention to the third chapter of The Book of Revelation, where we read that the Church of Laodicea in Asia Minor is in danger of being spewed or vomited out of the mouth of God, because of its lukewarmness. Christians at Laodicea, we are told, must therefore repent of their halfheartedness, or else face the painful consequences. More fundamentally, Christians must understand that God does not love without reproving (see Rev. 3:19). Jung, rather cynically, adds that "it would be quite understandable if the Laodiceans did not want too much of this 'love'."[23] And yet, Christians, down through the centuries, have at times been perfectly willing to settle for such a "love," as long as it contains the hope and promise of eternal consolation and protection.

Whether the context is Laodicea, the Protestant Reformation, or something more contemporary, a religious faith of quid pro quo usually mirrors the oedipal arrangement of early childhood: consolation and protection offered in exchange for unwavering obedience. Just as two functions—the function of accusation and punishment and the function of consolation and protection—intersected in the person of the oedipal father, so, too, we sometimes find the very same dual functions intersecting in the believer's image of God. In applying a Freudian hermeneutics of suspicion to the text of religious faith, Ricoeur has made a very important, albeit sobering discovery: religious believers sometimes do "prefer moral condemnation to the anguish of an existence that is both unprotected and unconsoled."[24] But believers, unlike the helpless child who must ultimately capitulate to the stronger oedipal father, have the capacity to imagine something better. We can either settle for an unreflective and insular religious faith of the first naïveté, or we can choose to expose our faith to a hermeneutics of suspicion, which invariably opens the door to a postcritical religious faith of the "second naïveté." This, as we will see in chapter 3, corresponds to what Rizzuto considers to be the supreme choice facing every person of faith, namely, whether or not to update and transform our psychical image of God.

■ FAITH AND PERSONAL TRANSFORMATION ■

In moving from an unexamined faith of the first naïveté to an updated and postcritical faith of the second naïveté, the religious believer will be undergoing nothing short of a psychical and spiritual transformation. This, make

is *grief + loss*

no mistake, heralds something of a warning: to move from a religious faith of the first naïveté, where God is virtually identical to the oedipal father, to a reconstructed faith of the second naïveté, where God is reimaged as the *unconditional* Giver of every good and perfect gift with no strings attached, implies internal change of momentous proportion. In many ways, what we are talking about is nothing short of a "conversion" experience, which makes the religious believer's reluctance to engage Freud and/or Ricoeur, if not desirable, then at least understandable. As Lewis Rambo has observed, in *Understanding Religious Conversion,* "all conversions implicitly require a leaving-behind or a reinterpretation of some past way of life and set of beliefs."[25] To put this in the language of Ricoeur, believers, in moving from a religious faith of the first naïveté to that of the second naïveté, will be undergoing something of a conversion experience, which, in terms of leaving behind some past way of life or past set of beliefs, means that they will be experiencing feelings of grief and loss.

These feelings of grief and loss, in the wake of parting with a faith of the first naïveté, cannot be underestimated or trivialized; they are real and palpable. Indeed, nothing, for the believer, will ever be the same again. This is why it should come as no surprise if even "mature" believers find themselves at times longing for the Edenic garden of simplicity and certainty, where God's consolation and protection were never once doubted. Nor should it be a surprise if the religious believer does not seem overjoyed at the prospect of exposing his or her faith to a Freudian hermeneutics of suspicion. What is important is that we help believers understand that what is involved in "converting" from a faith of the first naïveté to that of the second naïveté is, not a conversion to another God, but a conversion to a more authentic *image* of God. As we will see in chapter 3, this is precisely what Ana-Maria Rizzuto has in mind for Fiorella Domenico and Douglas O'Duffy, when she discusses the need for updating one's psychical God-image, making it more relevant to the life one is living now, as an adult.

For Ricoeur and, as we will see, for Rizzuto, not updating and transforming one's image of God, or refusing to convert from a religious faith of the first naïveté to that of the second naïveté, has its price: the perpetual arrestment of one's spiritual and emotional growth and development. Religious believers, in other words, can continue to feel perfectly consoled and protected by a powerful benevolent Providence, as long as they are willing to remain in a perpetual state of spiritual and emotional underdevelopment and/or a perpetual state of moral condemnation. The pain of moral condemnation, however, as Ricoeur has pointed out, seems easier to bear than the pain of an existence that is unprotected and unconsoled. The believer, then, is at least left with "a powerful being who rules over nature as an empire, who annuls death and redresses the afflictions of this life—if God is God this is all he can be; naïve religion is religion proper."[26]

Naive religion, or an unexamined religion of the first naïveté, is grounded, epistemologically, in what Ricoeur refers to as a "fraudulent totalization." With any fraudulent totalization, the pretentiousness of consciousness is readily apparent, as it seduces us into believing that we have been able to pull all the signs and symbols together into a coherent whole, and now have in our possession perfect and absolute knowledge. But this is little more than a static and stagnant *Bewusstsein*, or "being-consciousness," something that is hardly conducive to spiritual and emotional health and well-being. Ricoeur puts it this way:

> The impossibility of absolute knowledge . . . expresses the importance of fixing the criteriology of the divine in a closed system. Even if that advances step by step with the interpretation of historic signs, it is never completed. The testimonies of the absolute which rule the advance of self-consciousness give each time a new or more profound meaning to the divine. Also, the criteriology of the divine is likewise never finished. . . . The impossibility of absolute knowledge expresses the impotence of consciousness to bring all the signs together into a coherent whole. Tied to the testimony is the experience of "each time."[27]

The Western world has come to know, through the seminal work of Freud, that consciousness is an ongoing task, a *Bewusstwerden*, or "becoming-consciousness." And yet, we still find more than a few believers who profess a religious faith that presupposes that consciousness is essentially an end unto itself, a *Bewusstsein*. The believer, then, would seem to be saying, "If I think then I am," rather than, "If I think I must be becoming." Moreover, in terms of religious faith, "If I consciously think of God, then I must have the power to fix the criteriology of the divine in my own closed system." As a result, "God will always be there for me, ready to console and protect me as I see fit." This, according to Ricoeur, is nothing more than a fraudulent totalization.

Since consciousness, as Freud made abundantly clear, is never able to completely bring all the signs together into a coherent whole, and thus to avoid infinite regress and a perpetual state of ambiguity, religious believers may be tempted to settle for an arbitrary stopping-point. The arbitrary stopping-point centers on a powerful divine being who rules over nature, annuls death, and redresses the afflictions of an imperfect life. What is sobering is that the psyche of the postmodern individual is apparently not very different from that of the individual living at the dawn of Western civilization. Peter G. Ossorio, in his informative essay, "An Overview of Descriptive Psychology," situates the very same tendency to embrace fraudulent totalizations in the context of ancient Greece. He suggests that the quest for truth, whether carried out in the field of theology or psychology, is beset by some very serious problems, most notably "the problem of necessary but impossible foundations":

> In reflecting on the fact that all the common objects we see around us are held up by something, and evidently it is, ultimately, the world that holds everything else up, the Greeks were led to ask, "What holds the world up?" The answer, according to the myth, is that there is a giant called Atlas who holds the world on his shoulder. The answer is satisfactory for a time, until it sinks in that now there is a new problem, namely, "What holds Atlas up?" The answer is that Atlas is standing on the back of a huge elephant, and that is satisfying only briefly, because it is quickly apparent that this raises a new question, namely, "What holds the elephant up?" The answer, picturesquely enough, is that the elephant is standing on the back of a gigantic tortoise. But now immediately this raises the question, "What holds the tortoise up?" The answer is, "The tortoise is swimming in the eternal sea." Here the story ends, not because that is a satisfactory answer, but because one no longer knows what to say.[28]

Ricoeur would argue that the same could be said for a religious faith of the first naïveté, which grounds itself in the supposed reality of a powerful divine being who rules over nature, annuls death, and redresses our earthly sufferings. And here, at least for a faith of the first naïveté, the story reaches its end, not because we have arrived at a satisfactory answer, but because we no longer know what to say. Or, maybe the religious believer does know what to say, but, out of fear that a reimaged and postcritical faith of the second naïveté will not provide the same measure of divine consolation and protection, decides to settle for an arbitrary stopping-point where a perfectly consoled and protected existence is still a sure thing. The believer, then, at this point, would seem destined to remain a child forever. As Freud discovered, when the human individual reaches the decision that "he can never do without protection against strange superior powers, he lends those powers the features belonging to the figure of his father; he creates for himself gods whom he dreads, whom he seeks to propitiate, and whom he nevertheless entrusts with his own protection."[29]

Ricoeur wants us to understand that Freud's seminal and revolutionary discovery can actually and paradoxically propel the believer *beyond* a state of perpetual infantilization. Here is where we detect a slight teleological tone in Freud's writings, where even he, the self-described realist, begins to sound at least a little hopeful and optimistic. "Surely," he writes in *The Future of an Illusion*, "infantilization is destined to be surmounted," for human beings, in the end, "cannot remain children for ever."[30] Building on this Freudian hermeneutic, Ricoeur hopes to nudge the believer beyond a naive and infantile longing for eternal consolation and protection. What he would like, more than anything else, is for the religious believer to accept Freud's "education to reality," and, in so doing, move in the direction of a God who would not only have the attributes of "Providence," but would also surrender us "to the dangers of a life worthy of being called human."[31]

In reality, the religious believer has little to fear as the Freudian hermeneutics of suspicion peels away the unreflective layers of his or her faith. If the believer's religious faith, following the encounter with Freud, fails the test of authenticity—keep in mind that an unexamined faith of the first naïveté will *always* fail the test of authenticity—then surely it was hardly a faith the individual would have wanted in the first place. However, if the Freudian critique of religion peeled away more than an unreflective layer or two, if the believer's entire religious faith, top to bottom, was completely deconstructed and now stands in disarray, then the believer is about to experience a very rude and painful awakening. Whether the context be theological education, parish ministry, pastoral counseling, or spiritual direction, this is where religious believers might be tempted to shy away from an encounter with Freud, or, for that matter, with anyone else applying a hermeneutics of suspicion. Who of us, after all, relishes experiencing a faith crisis or a crisis of meaning, which an encounter with Freud cannot help but induce?

A crisis of faith or meaning, though, according to the social psychologist, Edward E. Sampson, is not always a bad thing. On the contrary, it could represent, as Ricoeur has already demonstrated, a valuable opportunity for spiritual growth and transformation. Sampson points out that "the transformation within our everyday life from one level of growth to another requires crisis, tension, and some transformation of the existing us by the newly emerging directions of our growth. . . . To be more blunt, there must be *major* personal disintegration before there can be any reintegration."[32] There must be, in other words, a certain amount of personal deconstruction before there can ever be any authentic growth and transformation. Again, to be quite honest, this implies internal change of momentous proportion. And since the ego needs and thrives on order, the individual cannot help but feel, when surrounded by disorder, like a fish out of water. Still, Ricoeur wants us to see that the order the ego has fashioned for itself is the real illusion, simply a fraudulent totalization designed to keep us from feeling the inherent ambiguities of human life. For "the cloak of the everyday standpoint" wraps itself around us, tighter and tighter, eventually blinding us to the ways "our lives have been pre-cast and determined."[33]

What could very well trouble the religious believer most about an anticipated engagement with Freud and his theory is that it has the potential for radical and decisive change. And change, no matter how beneficial it might be in the long run, is, at the time, rather unpleasant. Erik Erikson frequently witnessed the fear of change firsthand, noting that patients would "often resist care because it implies a change in ego identity, an ego resynthesis on the terms of changed economic history."[34] The same could be said of the believer, who, in conversing with Freud and psychoanalysis, must be willing to let go of one ego identity and begin the arduous task of rebuilding another. The new ego identity must necessarily include aspects of the id, which may make the believer even more anxious about the prospect of change. The Christian believer may find it difficult to even consider integrating aspects of the id into the self, when Scripture and theology are unambiguous about the dangers of the flesh and body. To be sure, the believer does have a theological warrant for avoiding an encounter with the id, particularly the familiar doctrine of original sin. After all, if it were not for, in theological terms, the desires of the flesh, or, in Freudian terms, the desires of the id, human beings, presumably, would still be enjoying paradise, otherwise known as the paradisial Garden of Eden.

In an attempt to re-create a more Edenic situation, believers may strive to wholeheartedly embrace the Pauline fruits of the Spirit. The familiar fruits or virtues—love, joy, peace, patience, kindness, goodness, faithfulness, gentleness and self-control (see Gal. 5:22-23)—are most certainly representative of the *spiritual side* of human existence. This normative model of Christian living, or, more accurately, of Christian perfection, however, leaves little room for embracing and integrating other aspects of our humanity, such as the instinctual forces of id. The believer, as already noted, is not always encouraged to integrate his or her biological desires, but is rather expected to triumph over them, and, in so doing, make restitution for the original sin of the human species. In the language of Christian theology, the spiritual side of the believer is expected to triumph emphatically over the flesh. In the language of psychoanalysis, the superego or the conscience is expected to hold sway over the biological forces of id. In Jungian terms, the spiritual side of the believer is expected to triumph over the shadow, that which contains the primitive forces of desire and instinct. Yet, as Jung never stopped reminding us, the brighter the persona of spiritual perfection, the more dangerous the shadow forces become.

Ricoeur, through the application of a Freudian hermeneutics of suspicion to the "text" of Christian theology, wants believers to know that it is time we turn the doctrine of original sin on its head. For centuries, Christian theology has taught us that the entire descent of Adam, even the unborn fetus in utero, is infected with the contagion known as original sin. What Ricoeur wants Christian believers to learn from Freud is that a more realistic description of our instinctuality may actually come from psychoanalysis. According to Ricoeur, we do not, after Freud, have to formulate our theology solely out of a feeling of guilt and remorse, in response to the original sin of a prehistoric human named Adam. Furthermore, we do not even need to despair of our instinctuality, for it, too, just like our spiritual side, is a gift from God. Ricoeur is especially uncomfortable with the traditional Christian formula that tends to indict humanity as a whole, for sins committed in the very distant, prehistoric past, while exonerating God. He would not go as far as Ludwig Feuerbach, or even Freud for that matter, and tell us to cease, once and for all, emptying ourselves into the heavens or into some transcendent "Wholly Other." Nevertheless, Ricoeur does urge us not to be hasty in condemning the human race as a whole, since this is yet another fraudulent totalization or arbitrary stopping-point.

Nor is it wise or advantageous to distance ourselves from our human and instinctual rootedness. "What psychoanalysis teaches us," Ricoeur points out in *The Conflict of Interpretations*, "is that we do not have to deny our desire; we can unmask it and recognize it."[35] Indeed, if we are in fact created *Imago Dei*, then this means *everything* about us reflects, in one form or another, our Creator. Psychoanalysis, then, serves as something of a corrective to an otherwise unbalanced and one-sided version of Christian theology, a version that seems intent on condemning the instinctual rootedness of humankind. This blanket condemnation is supposedly for our own good, since human desire, unchecked, will necessarily lead to disastrous consequences reminiscent of the debacle in the Garden of Eden. "We are here," Ricoeur writes, "at the source of the schema of *inheritance* which we have found at the basis of the Adamic speculation from St. Paul to St. Augustine to the present." He continues:

> But the meaning of this schema appears only if we completely renounce projecting the Adamic figure into history, only if we interpret it as a "type," "the type of the old man." We must not make the transition from myth to mythology. It will never be said enough just what evil has been done to Christianity by the literal interpretation, the "historicist" interpretation, of the Adamic myth. This interpretation has plunged Christianity into the profession of an absurd history and into pseudo-rational speculations on the quasi-biological transmission of a quasi-juridical guilt for the fault of an *other* man, back into the night of time, somewhere between Pithecanthropus and Neanderthal man. At the same time, the treasure hidden in the Adamic symbol has been squandered. . . . Between the naïve historicism of fundamentalism and the bloodless moralism of rationalism the way of the hermeneutics of symbols opens up.[36]

■ THE LIMITATIONS OF A FREUDIAN INTERPRETATION ■

Now Ricoeur thinks dialectically, so the archaeology of the human subject is only half of the hermeneutical equation, a necessary and indispensable part, to be sure, but still only one half. The second half of the hermeneutical equation is the hermeneutics of belief, or, more precisely, the hermeneutics of restored belief and meaning, purified by the refining fire of psychoanalysis. Toward that end, Ricoeur decides to juxtapose the realism of psychoanalysis with the idealism of Hegel's Absolute Spirit or Idea. Said another way, the Freudian *arche* or "archaeology" of the human subject becomes dialectically juxtaposed with a Hegelian telos or "teleology" of the Spirit. Neither of these alone, the arche or the telos, possesses sufficient interpretative power, but together, held firmly in dialectical tension, they point us toward what Ricoeur would call a "theology of hope."

This particular dialectic of the Freudian hermeneutics of suspicion held in tension with the Hegelian hermeneutics of progressive meaning, is not merely a clash of opposites or a dialectic *between* Freud and Hegel. Rather, "it is only when each interpretation is seen to be contained in the other that the antithetic is no longer simply the clash of opposites but the passage of each into the other. Only then is reflection truly in the archaeology and the archaeology in the teleology: reflection, teleology, and archaeology pass over into one another."[37] Put more simply, the *arche* of Freud and the telos of Hegel are understood together in the single act of interpretation. Following the refinement and strengthening of religious faith by the Freudian hermeneutics of suspicion, our attention will inevitably turn to the Hegelian hermeneutics of progressive meaning and to new and future possibilities for religious faith.

This is not a book on Hegel, so to delve more deeply into the Hegelian hermeneutics of progressive meaning would take us far afield. My purpose, however, in referring ever so briefly to Ricoeur's use of Hegelian theory, is to point out the inherent teleological limitations of Freudian theory. Freud, when it comes to religious faith, was largely a reductionist, which is simultaneously his great strength and weakness. Ricoeur also believes that the Freudian interpretation of religion is largely reductionistic; otherwise there would be little if any need to bring someone like Hegel into the discussion. Freud, according to Ricoeur, more than anyone else, can identify the neurotic and immature features of religious faith. But what happens next, after these features have been identified? Where does that leave us? How might we, as human beings and as religious believers, work our way out of this reductionistic solution?

For Freud, these questions are utterly moot. From the perspective of psychoanalysis, there is no reason to work our way out of this reductionistic situation, otherwise known as the human condition; recognition of our predicament is an end in itself. Recall Freud's words about Ananke, the reality of "harsh necessity," which demands from each of us simple resignation and acquiescence. There is, then, in the Freudian schema, no need to talk of the teleological dimension of religious faith or of a more mature and sophisticated religious faith characterized by purified belief and reconstructed meaning. Since religious faith retards the intellectual and emotional development of the individual and the species, why bother to talk of the teleological or progressive dimension of religious faith? Thus, Freud would think it oxymoronic to speak of *progressive* religion, as if there ever were or could be such a thing.

Freud, of course, is right, but only up to a point. Religious faith can be, at times, a regressive, rather than progressive phenomenon. However, the fact is that religious faith, particularly one that has been purified of its primitive naïveté, and has subsequently been reimaged and transformed, can bring new life and meaning to the believer. As Freud's "opponent," in *The Future of an Illusion*, argued, we human beings cannot live without our religious dreams and visions, unless we are willing to settle for an impoverished and stagnant way of living. This is what Rizzuto will make even more clear, when we get to her work in chapter 3: while Freud's solution for himself was a rather stark realism with no consolation except for the pride of being able to accept suffering without needing anyone or anything, this may not be the healthiest solution for the rest of us.

Whether we are religious believers or not, who of us really wants to live a life based on the overvaluation of material reality and the undervaluation or even, in the case of Freud, devaluation of psychical reality? And, even if we do have our empirical and scientific data, which tell us that because life is often harsh and unpredictable we look to religion to bring us a certain measure of hope and inspiration, what then? How do we make sense of the data? What do the data *mean*? For Freud, the data—life is harsh and unpredictable—mean nothing other than the fact that we human beings must accept life for *what it is*, rather than for what we would like it to be. But this is simply the repetition of the fallacy of scientism, that the empirical data or facts speak for themselves. As we know by now, however, or should know by now, thanks in part to the influential discipline of hermeneutics, empirical data *never* speak for themselves or stand on their own. They must *always* be interpreted.

Freud, to the very end, interpreted the data reductively—life is harsh and, consequently, we look to religion to give us a measure of hope and comfort. However, in his estimation, setting our sights on *what might be*, instead of simply accepting *what is*, amounts to a cop-out. But is religious faith always a cop-out, always a means of psychical escape from the pressures of harsh reality? Sometimes, but not always. Some of us prefer a more balanced solution, one that holds the regressive and teleological dimensions of religious faith firmly in dialectical tension. Moreover, we want a more creative and imaginative solution, something more than a stark realism, which offers little in the way of hope and consolation. Freud, at the end of *Civilization and Its Discontents*, informs us that he has nothing hopeful to offer the human individual: "I have not the courage to rise up before my fellow-men as a prophet, and I bow to their reproach that I can offer them no consolation. . . ."[38] Thus, it is hardly a surprise that Ricoeur, who does value the human capacity to create new meaning, to dream new dreams, and to imagine more hopeful visions, must eventually look *beyond* Freud for a more progressive, teleological solution.

Human beings simply cannot live on the bread of material reality alone, nor should they be expected to. Freud, with his hermeneutics of suspicion, has been a skillful guide up until now, up until this particular point of our hermeneutical journey. Religious faith has passed through the fire of the Freudian critique of religion, and has been purified of its primitive naïveté. But now we must look beyond Freud, to the hermeneutics of restored belief and meaning, in order to forge a more creative and imaginative solution. Ricoeur adds:

> This philosophical investigation into the religious meaning of [Freudian] atheism has led us from resignation to consent and from consent to a mode of dwelling on earth that is governed by poetry and thought. This mode of being is no longer "the love of fate" but a love of creation. Such a fact suggests a movement from atheism toward faith. The love of creation is a form of consolation which depends on no external compensation and which is equally remote from any form of vengeance. Love finds within itself its own compensation; it is itself consolation.[39]

Ricoeur, as we have learned, primarily follows the Hegelian hermeneutics of progressive meaning, as a way of pointing us beyond Freud's reductive "love of fate," to a more dynamic love of creation. He also looks to Søren Kierkegaard, specifically, to the Kierkegaardian "passion for the possible," which, "in contrast to all wisdom of the present, to all submission to necessity, underscores the imprint of the promise on freedom."[40] Through this passion for new and creative solutions and possibilities, hope is grafted onto Ananke, onto "harsh necessity," enabling us to move from mere resignation and mere acceptance of fate to a more creative mode of dwelling on the earth. It is creation, rather than fate, which we must now embrace, especially if we desire something more than a stark realism that offers nothing more than the pride of being able to accept our fate without attaching ourselves to anything or anyone.

If Freud's love-of-fate solution to the human predicament is all that we can hope for, then it is really pointless for the believer to exchange an unexamined faith of the first naïveté for a transformed faith of the second naïveté. But a Freudian hermeneutics of suspicion is not an end unto itself; it is the *means* to the end of finding a more creative mode of dwelling on the earth. Again, with Kierkegaard in mind, Ricoeur reminds us that "freedom entrusted to the 'God who comes,' is open to the radically new; it is the creative imagination of the possible."[41] We come face-to-face with the supreme limitation of Freudian theory: it is not open to radically new possibilities. Instead, the Freudian hermeneutics of suspicion focuses exclusively on the repetition of the past or on the return of the repressed.

Not that Ricoeur gives up trying to find some teleological dimension within the Freudian corpus. He argues that while psychoanalysis does have an explicit reductive dimension to it, it also has an implicit teleological dimension. Ricoeur informs us that we need only remember that consciousness for Freud is a progressive task, a *Bewusstwerden* or "becoming-consciousness." Thus, Freud can say that Leonardo da Vinci was "a man who has begun to have an inkling of the grandeur of the universe with all its complexities and its laws," that he "is a part of those active forces and that in accordance with the scale of his personal strength the way is open for him to try to alter a small portion of the destined course of the world—a world in which the small is no less wonderful and significant than the great."[42] This passage, Ricoeur believes, taken from the book on da Vinci, is illustrative of the "other side" of Freud, the implicit teleological side that can balance Freud's overt and explicit reductive side. For Ricoeur, this work on da Vinci illustrates that "Freud's philosophical temperament consists perhaps in this delicate equilibrium—or subtle conflict?—between lucidity free of illusion and the love of life."[43]

Psychoanalysis, then, which directly reflects the temperament of its creator, would also consist in the very same delicate equilibrium, between reality free of illusion and the love of life, between necessity and possibility. Ricoeur is convinced that in light of Freud's observation about da Vinci, that Leonardo could in fact alter a small portion of the destined course of the world, explicit necessity and implicit possibility delicately coexist within Freud's mind and within his theory. Maybe so, but it does appear to be something of a stretch. Ricoeur has presented such a compelling and convincing case for the reductive power of a Freudian hermeneutic that his comments on the implicit telos in psychoanalysis seem to be something of an afterthought.

What Ricoeur does best is challenge the religious believer to genuinely feel the dialectical tension between psychoanalysis and religious faith. It would therefore make more sense, methodologically, to simply let the Freudian hermeneutics of suspicion be just that, the *hermeneutics of suspicion*, without feeling the need to find a teleological needle in the haystack. Ricoeur may very well believe that finding a teleological dimension within psychoanalytic theory is a necessary prerequisite to getting the religious believer to at least consider engaging Freud and his theory of religion. And he might be right, especially within certain Christian faith communities. In other Christian communities, however, it may be enough to simply let Freud be Freud, without feeling obligated to dress him up.

Ricoeur's dialectic is most convincing and persuasive when he selects *a* representative of the hermeneutics of suspicion—Freud—and *a* representative of the hermeneutics of belief or meaning—Hegel. This way, there can be genuine dialectical tension, in that the believer can listen to and learn from psychoanalysis as it informs, critiques, and ultimately strengthens one's religious faith. Then, in turn, a hermeneutics of restored belief reforms our understanding of the hermeneutics of suspicion. Freud, of course, would be more comfortable with this approach, since he himself maintained to the very end that he had nothing prescriptive and teleological to offer either the believer or unbeliever, above and beyond mere resignation to Ananke.

Ricoeur rightly points out that "we are bound to agree that any articulation of faith must pass through and beyond the 'hermeneutics of suspicion,' not slide around it."[44] This is especially important today, when, in response to the annual loss of millions of mainline church members, the religious community feels pressured and hurried to articulate a hermeneutics of restored belief and meaning. In the rush to put forward a compelling theological agenda, however, there is the danger that we will merely pass *around* but not *through* the influential Freudian hermeneutics of suspicion. To put this another way, believers might be tempted to get from Point A, the first naïveté of religious faith, to Point C, the second naïveté of restored theological meaning, by merely passing around but not through Point B, the Freudian hermeneutics of suspicion. But if the religious faith of believers is not first refined by a thoroughgoing hermeneutics of suspicion, then the reality is that despite appearances, their faith will remain of an unreflective nature, unable to meet the demands of a postmodern world.

What many religious believers will inevitably want to know is this: What will I learn from Freud, if I decide to heed Ricoeur's advice and have an extensive conversation with psychoanalysis? The answer, to a large extent, is that Freud's schooling will force us to recognize that while God exists *out there,* transcendent of time and space, God also exists *in here,* inside the psyche of the human individual, juxtaposed with the psychical images of parents and other important cultural representatives and influences. As Rizzuto will make even more clear in chapter 3, our ignorance of God's psychical role means that we are overlooking important and relevant data having to do with our individual and collective developmental history. Put in the context of pastoral care, it means that clergy, chaplains, pastoral counselors, spiritual directors, and seminary faculty are missing important and vital pieces of information about the developmental history of those in their care. Freud's schooling, therefore, teaches us that the "text" of human consciousness and the "text" of religious faith are never, even under the most progressive set of circumstances, entirely divorced from the archaic and primitive layers of the psyche.

For Ricoeur, the fundamental question is, "Does the affective dynamism of religious belief have the wherewithal to *overcome* its own archaism?"[45] To genuinely answer the question in the affirmative is to recognize, once and for all, that our religious faith must be subjected to a process of interpretation and reinterpretation, and that "such a process must be repeated again and again in particular contexts if it is to be a critical reflection, empowering heritage, and liberating vision. . . ."[46] Religious faith, Ricoeur argues, cannot be satisfied anymore with the mere repetition of its origins, certainly not after it has come in contact with psychoanalysis. Instead, it must accept the challenge posed by Freud, in order to become more than it has ever been before.

What Ricoeur wants us to recognize is that psychoanalysis is a "gift" for all, even for the religious believer. Though it is by nature reductionistic and deconstructive, it is still a liberating force for authentic change, growth, and transformation. The believer, as Ricoeur has made very clear, is obligated to converse with Freudian theory, which has the capacity to enlarge our field of consciousness, strengthen our religious faith, and ultimately free us for a new reign of truthfulness and authenticity. Ricoeur reminds us that "psychoanalysis never confronts one with bare forces, but always with forces in search of meaning."[47] This is what Ricoeur refers to as the "semantics of desire." Therefore, the "gift" of psychoanalysis is an "ever richer and more articulated interiority,"[48] which will, in turn, point us toward an ever richer and more clearly articulated religious faith. The paradox is that Freud helps us see what a religious faith of the future should and should not look like, even though he himself believed that religion had no future. Ricoeur would agree with Freud's prediction, as long as it applies to a religious faith of the first naïveté, one that is dependent on an oedipal Deity.

Some of us, who are still mourning the death of the oedipal god of consolation and constraint, may not readily agree with Ricoeur, let alone with Freud. For even in the postmodern believer of the Western world, "there confront one another an adult critic and a naive child who listen to the Word."[49] But sooner or later, particularly in this complicated postmodern world, believers will have to move beyond the innocence of the first naïveté of faith to the reflectiveness of the second naïveté, the latter having been refined and strengthened by a Freudian hermeneutics of suspicion. In terms of our individual and collective development, it is really only a matter of time. Ricoeur writes,

> It seems to me that only one path has been decisively closed off, that of an onto-theology which culminates in the idea of a moral god, conceived as the origin and foundation of an ethics of prohibition and condemnation. I believe that we are henceforth incapable of returning to an order of moral life which would take the form of a simple submission to commandments or to an alien or supreme will, even if this will were represented as divine. We must accept as a positive good the critique of ethics and religion that has been undertaken by the school of suspicion. From it we have learned to understand that the commandment that gives death, not life, is a product and projection of our own weakness.[50]

■ T H R E E ■

The Psychical Role Of God

How can therapy be of help here? It cannot give us back our lost childhood, nor can it change the past facts. No one can heal by maintaining
or fostering illusion. The paradise of preambivalent harmony, for which
so many patients hope, is unattainable. But the experience of one's own
truth, and the postambivalent knowledge of it, make it possible to return to one's own world of feelings at an adult level—without paradise,
but with the ability to mourn.

Alice Miller, *The Drama of the Gifted Child*

What becomes apparent, as we continue working our way through the chapters of critical analysis, is that each of these theorists approaches Freud and his theory of religion dialectically, nei-ther embracing the totality of his theory nor completely dismissing it. These chapters, then, do *not* form an either-or critique of Freud and religious faith, which means that the chapters, and the theorists we meet therein, are not altogether dismissive of Freudian theory. We have already seen how Paul Ricoeur, a philosopher and theologian, works within the dialectical tension between Freud and faith. But how do others, who work in very different fields, go about holding Freud and religion in tension?

The psychoanalyst, Ana-Maria Rizzuto, for example, in the epilogue of her groundbreaking book, *The Birth of the Living God*, explains that "in the end I had to disagree with Freud—but not totally: only with one Freud, the one of science, intellect, and reality, the Freud who said, 'No, our science is no illusion. But an illusion it would be to suppose that what science cannot give us we can get elsewhere.' The Freud who *believes* that man lives on the bread of knowledge alone I have to disagree with." But Rizzuto does not leave the matter there, for she goes on to say that she also follows "the other Freud, the Freud of object relations, the Oedipus Complex, family relations, until through my research I arrive at one of his own conclusions about some individuals in the Western world: 'The idea of a single great god—an idea

75

which must be recognized as a completely justified memory . . . has a compulsive character: it *must* be believed'. . . ."[1]

Rizzuto will flesh out for us, in this chapter, her dialectical approach to Freud, and her conviction that God is not only a transcendent, external reality, but also a more immanent psychical reality. In fact, she calls our attention to the methodological "ground rules" of her investigation, pointing out, in the introduction to *The Birth of the Living God*, that "questions about the actual existence of God do not pertain here," for "my method enables me to deal only with psychic experiences." Therefore, she continues, "logic does not permit me to go beyond a psychological level of inference."[2] As much as I admire Rizzuto and respect her work on Freud and religious faith, I find this an interesting, if not unfortunate choice of words. Had she written, "My *methodology* does not permit me to go beyond a psychological level of inference," rather than "*logic* does not permit me . . . ," she would have been further ahead. To suggest that logic does not permit us going beyond a psychological level of inference, into the theological realm of transcendent reality, that one must keep psychology methodologically separate from theology, betrays a *personal* logic, which may make perfect sense to the psychologist who subscribes to it but less sense to someone else, like the theologian.

Rizzuto's method of dealing solely with psychical experience is reminiscent of a Jungian approach to the phenomenon of religious faith. "It would be a regrettable mistake," wrote C. G. Jung, "if anybody should understand my observations to be a kind of proof of the [actual] existence of God," for "they prove only the existence of an archetypal image of the Deity, which to my mind is the most we can assert psychologically about God."[3] This form of "logic" is what puzzles, if not infuriates certain theologians and philosophers. Martin Buber, for example, responded to this position taken by Jung, and his response could just as easily be directed at Rizzuto's approach: "This means, in effect, that the possibility is not left open that God—who, if the singular and exclusive word 'God' is not to lose all meaning, cannot be limited to a single mode of existence as if it were only a question of one among many gods—exists independent of as well as related to the human subject."[4] It may seem strange, therefore, that a theorist selected to critique Freud's dogmatic, either-or position on religious faith may also be somewhat guilty of adopting a similar either-or attitude: the scholar of religion, so the thinking goes, must situate herself, methodologically, within either a psychological or a theological framework; one or the other, but not both.

While I feel obligated to point out Rizzuto's methodological shortsightedness, I also want to say, with just as much conviction, that it will not take anything away from her critique of Freud and his theory of religion. She admits that her study of religious faith, in *The Birth of the Living God*, will not go beyond the bounds of the psychological level, but in terms of critiquing Freudian theory, this is more than apropos since Freud believed that religious faith amounted to nothing more than psychological projection. In other words, because Freud concluded that God is nothing more than a psychical product, a study of religious faith, like Rizzuto's, which is limited to "a psychological level of inference," is still very applicable to a critique of Freudian theory. As we will see, Rizzuto, in her later book, *Why Did Freud Reject God?* takes a less neutral position toward faith and unbelief. She will suggest, for example, that because of the absence of emotional attachment with his earliest caregivers, Freud was necessarily predisposed to be an unbeliever.

This chapter, then, featuring the work of a psychoanalyst and object relations theorist, will be divided into two parts. The first part will begin with the "other Freud," the Freud of object relations, the Oedipus Complex, and family relations, the Freud with whom Rizzuto completely agrees. After examining Rizzuto's work on religious faith, particularly the data from her clinical case studies, we will be hard-pressed not to admit that the "other Freud" did manage to identify something consequential when he theorized that God is an exaltation of parental imagoes. Conversely, the latter portion of the chapter will focus on the Freud of science, intellect, and reality, the Freud who believed that human beings must live on the bread of scientific and empirical knowledge alone. Specifically, the second part of the chapter will explore the intimate and inextricable connection, in Freudian theory, between the relegation of God to the psychical realm and the simultaneous devaluation of psychical space as a lesser reality. To be sure, one cannot underestimate the importance of object relations theory as a corrective to classical Freudian theory, especially when it comes to the realm of psychical space, the realm of creativity, imagination, reimagination, and grace.

■ THE FREUD OF OBJECT RELATIONS, THE OEDIPUS COMPLEX, AND FAMILY RELATIONS ■

The great strength of Rizzuto's research lies in her clinical specificity, or what she describes as her "clinical method." Obviously, she is vulnerable to the criticism that her work lacks empirical specificity, yet she remains unfazed. While giving empirical researchers of religious faith, like Benjamin Beit-Hallahmi and Michael Argyle, their due, and agreeing that "empirical studies can help us generalize some findings by statistical validation," she warns that "such conclusions, however, not only lack clinical specificity but may be deleterious to good clinical work if applied indiscriminately." She continues:

> A statement, for example, that "the findings of a relationship between the image of God and the image of the opposite-sex or preferred parent lend support to the notion that the deity is a projected love-object" may be statistically correct, but it does not do justice to large numbers of patients who have very complex and painful relations with their Gods. For the psychoanalyst the facts about a person's God need to be personalized and specific to be understood.[5]

Nor, I would argue, is it a coincidence that this is the point of view of a *female* researcher. Rizzuto, like many other female clinicians, theorists, and researchers, believes that empirical studies, while providing us with a starting point for a discussion of religious faith, do not do justice to the personhood of the *individual* believer or client, a distinct and concrete person living and struggling in the here and now of human history. As Miriam Greenspan notes, in *A New Approach to Women and Therapy,* the empirical researcher, as opposed to the clinician, is supposedly the real expert or the real scientist, "a detached, neutral, benignly disinterested observer" of human behavior and the human condition. This attitude of disinterested observation, whether it be manifested in the field of psychology, religion, or the natural sciences, is part and parcel of the scientific method, but, adds Greenspan, the notion that "objectivity is equivalent to disinterested observation . . . is all the more dubious where the object of measurement is a person engaged in a relationship with another person, and the goal of that relationship is to alleviate the first person's emotional distress."[6] Greenspan happens to be addressing the subject of psychotherapy, but her argument could just as well be applied to the study and understanding of religion and spirituality. For example, it is not too difficult to see that religious faith is an equally intimate and personal phenomenon, where the object of measurement is an individual engaged in a relationship with his or her God, and one of the goals of this relationship is to lessen the person's emotional and spiritual distress.

Rizzuto, in attempting to do justice to those patients who come to her with very complex and painful relations with their God, shares with us the case of Fiorella Domenico, a woman entering her sixties who "illustrates in every detail Freud's description of the derivation of religion from the oedipal conflict and its magnification to the divine sphere."[7] Fiorella represents what Rizzuto describes as the first category of religious faith, which is made up of those individuals who have believed in God all their lives, never once questioning their God's existence. This, as we saw in chapter 2, corresponds to Ricoeur's "first naïveté" of religious faith, a faith that has never been subjected to the test of critical reflection. Rizzuto uses similar terminology, when she describes, in general, the first category of religious faith, and, in particular, the psychical image of God belonging to Fiorella: "This type of [God] representation has not undergone serious conceptual reelaboration in early or late adolescence," but rather coincides with "the type of representation used by a child of the latency period: namely, it is free of contradictions, pain, or intellectual questioning and colored by an uncomplicated naïveté."[8] Fiorella's God, therefore, is a rather domesticated and lifeless deity, hardly the same God who had the power to shake the mountain at Sinai, in the presence of the Hebrews.

But what could possibly compel Fiorella, as well as others with a God-image colored by an uncomplicated naïveté, to settle for such a tame and simplistic religious faith? For Rizzuto, no one can answer the question better than Freud. Fiorella, we learn, grew up in a small New England city, the second child of blue-collar, Italian immigrants. Her family, she told Rizzuto, was very traditional: her emotionally reserved father, though he worked long hours away from home, was still the unquestioned head of the home, while her emotionally volatile mother ran the household. Rizzuto points out that Fiorella, in typical oedipal fashion, felt intensely ambivalent about her mother, especially from the age of six on, while experiencing feelings of comfort and security, when in her father's presence. The phrase, *from the age of six on*, is very telling, for it just so happens to correspond precisely with the period of transition between, in Freudian psychosexual terminology, the end of the oedipal phase of development and the beginning of the latency stage.

Fiorella, in describing her preschool years to Rizzuto, intimated that it was her mother she felt closest to until, at around the age of six, she began to resent her mother's angry tirades and heavy-handedness. She found herself gravitating, emotionally, toward her father, even though he was an aloof and quiet individual. Furthermore, Fiorella's devotion to her father, from the age of six to the age of thirty-eight—the year of his death—never seemed to wane, despite the fact that by age thirty-eight she had been married twenty years. Her husband, though, as Rizzuto learned during the course of Fiorella's treatment, was in many ways a carbon copy of her father. Indeed, in getting married at the age of eighteen, in moving directly from her family-of-origin home to that of her husband, without any time in between to forge an identity of her own, Fiorella had little time and opportunity to separate, psychically, her family of origin from her more immediate family. Consequently, Rizzuto concludes that the father and husband "were in a relation of direct continuity in [Fiorella's] mind."[9] It is not a coincidence, then, that Fiorella would reveal to Rizzuto that *after* the death of her father, not to mention after twenty years of marriage, her husband could finally become the most important man in her life. "She had no need," writes Rizzuto, "to overcome her post-oedipal attachment and could go without transition or disruption from loving her father to loving her husband."[10]

This direct continuity of affect or emotionality is illustrated by Fiorella's attitude toward the passing of her parents. While she reported feeling sad at the death of her parents—her father and mother died within two years of each other—Fiorella could still find sufficient solace and consolation in the presence of her husband, the recipient of Fiorella's redirected love. However, following a terrifying night when her husband had an excruciating attack of kidney stones, and when her telephone calls for help and assistance went either unanswered or unheeded, Fiorella began to doubt, *for the first time*, whether all was right with the world and whether she could count on being protected from the pitiless forces of nature. Rizzuto eventually diagnosed Fiorella as suffering from an anxiety disorder, in response to the fear of abandonment or what Freud termed *a fear of loss of love*.

Freud, writing in *Civilization and Its Discontents*, noted that if someone "loses the love of another person upon whom he is dependent, he also ceases to be protected from a variety of dangers."[11] Even the danger of death, that is, the death of her own parents and especially the death of the person she loved most, namely, her father, could not faze Fiorella *as long as* she had a "backup" in the person of her husband. But when questions about his health began to surface, following the ordeal with the kidney stones, she had to face the possibility that she might outlive him. Who would look out for her then, when both father and husband were gone, when there was no longer a direct continuity of affect? Fiorella, in theory, could become a widow at any moment, which, on the surface, would leave her feeling as if she had been abandoned by a husband. More significant, however, was what she was experiencing below the surface, outside the bounds of conscious awareness: the feeling of being abandoned by the psychical objects and images that heretofore had given her a measure of peace and serenity.

By now, the reader may be asking, "What about God?" True, Fiorella fears the imminent loss of her husband and, by association, the direct continuity of emotional attachment to her father, but might not God or her image of God fill, if not all the empty void, then at least a portion of it? Fiorella, after all, had been born, christened, and raised in the church, had attended Mass daily for much of her life, and, even now in her sixties, was still a very devout Roman Catholic believer. So, even if her husband were to die anytime soon, leaving her a widow, she would technically not be alone, for surely her God would be there to protect and console her through the coming weeks and months of the grieving process.

Fiorella informed Rizzuto that she always felt close to God, even during the more difficult times of her life. In describing her relationship with God, on a questionnaire she had filled out during the treatment, Fiorella wrote, "I have never changed my thinking about God because I have always loved him," "I like everything about God," and "I never felt distant from God because I feel he is always with us."[12] Thus, if God has always been Fiorella's help in ages past, why not now? Why, all of a sudden, has her husband's health and the prospect of his death filled her with such feelings of dread and helplessness? While his death would trigger, in Fiorella, feelings of grief and pain and disappointment, it would not, or so we might think, signal the end of the world or the end of her relationship with God. Or would it?

Rizzuto asked Fiorella, at one point during the treatment, to get very specific and try pinpointing the actual beginning of this intimate relationship with God. In response, Fiorella, with instant recall, indicated that she began to feel especially close to God at around the age of six or seven. She said, "The time of my life when I felt the closest to God was when I passed my first Communion and was seven years old because I was beginning to understand God."[13] On a surface level, this can be taken easily enough at face value—Fiorella's love for, and devotion to, God stems from the impressive experience of a first Communion. But if Freud has taught us anything, it is that there is always more than meets the eye. Said another way, any human experience, whether cognitive, affective, or behavioral, or a combination of any of these, is pregnant with meaning on multiple levels. Freud, in his magnum opus, *The Interpretation of Dreams* (1900), had observed that when it comes to dreaming there is always the *manifest* content and the *latent* content, the former being the portion of the dream we remember upon awakening and the latter being the unconscious meaning concealed behind the more obvious surface content. Similarly, Fiorella's devotion to God, on a manifest level, simply stems from the joy of receiving a first Communion. But, to Rizzuto, who has the trained ear and eye of a psychoanalyst, there is always the unconscious latent content that is being concealed or hidden behind the more respectable manifest interpretation.

Fiorella consciously and quite honestly believes that her love and devotion for God grew out of the experience of a first Communion, which, as far as Rizzuto is concerned, is true on a manifest level of interpretation. But what, we may ask, is Fiorella's emotional or spiritual truth at a deeper level, at the latent level of interpretation? According to Rizzuto, it is a fact of no small importance that Fiorella's love for God began to take shape around the age of six or seven, for this "is also the time when she consciously began to prefer her father over her mother."[14] Her involvement, at the time, in a first Communion is really rather incidental, in light of the powerful and formative emotional forces at work in her family of origin and the way in which she arranged and ordered those forces within her psyche. It just so happens that at the age of seven Fiorella began to distance herself emotionally from her mother, began to feel very ambivalent about her mother, and instead began looking to her father for emotional warmth and comfort. This she consistently got from him, as long as he was alive. Fiorella, up until the age of thirty-eight—the year of her father's death—could rest assured that all was right with her personal world, that she had all the love and comfort she needed. Even when her father died, she still clung to the conviction that all was right with the world, because of the transference or the direct continuity of emotional attachment from father to husband.

Fiorella never once—at least not until her husband's sudden attack of kidney stones and the terrifying prospect of his death—felt the need to question the existence of a benevolent Providence, and whether that Providence would, at certain times, cause her to be the plaything of the mighty and pitiless forces of nature. If Providence did not prevent Fiorella and her husband from becoming the playthings of nature, at the time of his illness, who is to say that Providence will not, in a seeming spirit of capriciousness, will it to happen again and again? Fiorella's universe, therefore, was no longer predictable. Up until this point of her life, she could and did fall back upon her psychical image of God as a source of consolation and protection. Now, however, because her God-image carried so much oedipal baggage, so much continuity of affect with a deceased father and a convalescent husband, she was suddenly left out in the cold of a cruel and unpredictable universe. As we learned earlier, Freud had observed from his clinical work with patients that a most intimate connection exists, psychically, between a perceived loss of love and a perceived loss of protection:

This, however, is easily explained by the original infantile stage of conscience, which, as we see, is not given up after the introjection into the superego, but persists alongside of it and behind it. Fate is regarded as a substitute for the parental agency. If a man is unfortunate it means he is no longer loved by this highest power; and, threatened by such a loss of love, he once more bows to the parental representative in his superego—a representation whom, in his days of good fortune, he was ready to neglect. This becomes especially clear where Fate is looked upon in the strictly religious sense of being nothing else than an expression of the Divine Will.[15]

As long as Fate or Providence did not cause Fiorella to be the plaything of the pitiless forces of nature, and her days were filled with the good fortune of direct continuity with the affect of her childhood, all was well. But as soon as the continuity of affect was threatened, as soon as the severing of the psychical lifeline to the object relations of her childhood became a real and frightening possibility, Fiorella no longer had internal resources to fall back upon. And, again, we may still be left wondering what kept Fiorella, even in the face of adversity, from affirming the steadfast love and presence of her God? While her God-image did betray an association with the object relations of the oedipal period of development, and while that psychical image of God was beginning to break down, there was nothing preventing her from reaching out to the actual and transcendent God of the universe.

I once had a conversation with a seminary classmate about this very issue, only in the context of imaging God as masculine or feminine. This seminarian, a woman, was very annoyed at certain "feminists" in our class, who had told her that because they had been raised by emotionally and/or physically abusive fathers, they would never be able, hard as they try, to image God as Father. My classmate was troubled by the logic of these feminists, because she believed that since God the Father was nothing like an abusive earthly father, they should be able to image a divine Father without too much difficulty. And yet, here is where we encounter a fundamental truth, something that we have learned from Freud and seen illustrated in Rizzuto's clinical data: an external and transcendent God, who exists beyond time and space, can *never* be entirely imaged or reimaged in the minds of religious believers separate from the parental images and representations formed in the early years of childhood.

These feminists, then, were not just being, as my classmate claimed, obstinate and rebellious; they had a point. If God can *only* be imaged as a heavenly Father or reimaged as a more benevolent Father, then that image, no matter how revised or updated, will still be the bearer of residual traces of an abusive father of childhood. Therefore, if these feminists are to believe in a kind and loving God, they will, out of necessity, need to image or reimage God as something *other than* or *more than* Father, as, say, Mother, Friend, Brother, or Sister. This is the Freudian lesson, and it certainly appears irrefutable: God and one's parents are never entirely separate from each other, psychically, even when the early caregivers nurture rather than abuse. God, to be sure, exists "out there," but God also, as Freud and Rizzuto have both cogently demonstrated, exists "in here."

Fiorella did have a warm and loving father, even if he was emotionally reserved, so she would have a better chance of reimaging God in the form of another Father. Still, this would be no easy task, for she would need to exchange a God of the pleasure principle for a God of the reality principle, an omnipotent God who would never, under any circumstances, force her to be a plaything of the forces of nature for a God who does not always intervene to rescue her from every difficult and threatening situation. "One might suppose," Freud wrote in *The Future of an Illusion*, "that this condition of things would result in a permanent state of anxious expectation. . . ."[16] Sure enough, this permanent state of anxious expectation, in response to the sudden unpredictability of the universe, is what brought Fiorella into treatment in the first place.

Fiorella's psychical God-image, rooted in the oedipal and postoedipal period of development, could no longer sustain her, emotionally and spiritually, through the vicissitudes of human life. If anything, her God-image, in the face of threatening circumstances, may go from one extreme to the other, from a warm and benevolent Providence to a capricious and unpredictable God of wrath and punishment. The chief use of Fiorella's God-image, then, prior to her psychiatric treatment, was

> in perpetuating her relationship with her father, that is, keeping the admired protector in a satisfying relation of caring love, in a simplified universe ruled like a harmonious household. . . . She had no need to overcome her post-oedipal attachment and could go without transition or disruption from loving her father to loving her husband, well guided by her intense repression.[17]

What is evident is that a triangular continuity of affect exists in Fiorella's psyche, between her father, husband, and God. As long as divine love and protection were guaranteed, in the concrete manifestation of a *healthy* father or husband, Fiorella had no need to doubt or question the existence of a benevolent Providence. Traces of her God, or the "footprints in the sand," were all around her, first in the person of her father, then later in the person of her husband. However, the threat of her husband's death brought to her immediate attention the possibility that she would soon be bereft of the concrete manifestation of divine love and protection. For someone like Fiorella, whose God-image never developed beyond what it was at the end of the oedipal stage, this is really too much to bear. To put this another way, it is no wonder that Fiorella, in the face of her husband's declining health, was overcome by a wave of anxiety, for if he were to die on her, she would be losing, all at once, a husband, a father and a God. Rizzuto summarizes the case of Fiorella this way, in her essay, "The Psychological Foundations of Belief in God:"

> In [The Birth of the Living God]. . . . I found a peaceful and joyful believer, Fiorella Domenico, who is in love with a God who is "great" and who "watches over us." When the tragedies of life confronted her naive enthusiasm about her God, she solved the dilemma by developing a phobia . . . that protected her God, her love for him, and also her need to update her girlish representation of God to a God capable of handling contradiction and suffering.[18]

Fiorella's psychical image or representation of God would seem to confirm Freud's fundamental hypothesis: a personal God is, psychologically, an exalted earthly father. Or, if these words strike us as absolutist, then we may wish to modify the statement, having it read, in regard to the case of Fiorella, that "a personal God is at least a partially exalted father." If, however, our goal is to be completely objective, then we are left with no alternative: Fiorella's personal God is in fact little more than an exalted father. Interestingly enough, Freud went on to say, immediately after making the brash statement that God is nothing other than an exalted father, that this particular finding "brings us evidence every day of how young people lose their religious beliefs as soon as their father's authority breaks down."[19] Just like the rebellious adolescent who for the first time begins to experience the psychical breakdown of parental influence and authority, Fiorella, likewise, was experiencing the painful psychical collapse of her beloved father's authority.

Fiorella, though, was far removed, chronologically and emotionally, from adolescence, for, as we see from her case study, she had no interest whatsoever in forming an identity she could call her own. In fact, her anxiety and phobias were something of a defensive maneuver, intended, as Rizzuto observes, to ward off or keep at bay the need to update her underdeveloped representation of God and to transform it into an image capable of handling contradictions and suffering. This—the updating of her psychical image of God—was what Fiorella *needed*, but certainly not what she *wanted*. She had managed to get around the issue of identity formation once before, during adolescence and early adulthood (she married at the age of eighteen), and she would, through various defensive maneuvers of an intrapsychic nature, manage to get around it again. "Developmentally," writes Rizzuto, "her elaboration of the God representation stopped there: Her adolescence bypassed the crisis with authority figures by adopting, without question, her parents' morality and ideals. She did not go through the normal crisis of doubting and disbelief which so deeply troubles the religious conscience of adolescents."[20]

What the case of Fiorella confirms is that the Freud of object relations, the Oedipus Complex, and family relations did in fact make an important and seminal discovery: there *is* an intimate and inextricable psychical connection between parental imagoes and images of God. How could it be otherwise, when, as we have seen with Fiorella, the parental imagoes are indestructible, exerting a lasting influence for the duration of a person's life? Freud had theorized, with his first topography of the human psyche, that when it comes to the realm of unconsciousness, where those imagoes formed in the early days of childhood reside, we are entering a world that is *zeitlos* or "timeless." The parental standards and values that we introjected and internalized unconsciously, while we were still young children, will always, to the end of our days, impact and influence all later relationships with God and with other human beings. This is the view of the "other Freud," the one with whom Rizzuto completely agrees. It is this Freud who was attentive to the intimate connection between one's God-image and one's parental imagoes, as well as "the lifelong influence of the parental imagoes, their indestructibility, and their transformation under the impact of new people we encounter in life."[21]

Freud, then, was at least partially correct, which means that when we avoid him at all costs, we, as Rizzuto has pointed out, run the risk of ignoring the psychical role of God in an individual's life and of missing an important and relevant piece of information about the person's developmental history. However, while Freud had much to say about the lifelong influence of parental imagoes, including their indestructibility and their intimate connection with an individual's God-image, he had far less to say about the process of updating and transforming our God-image, primarily because of, in general, his devaluation of psychical space, and, in particular, his devaluation of preoedipal experience and the oceanic feeling of oneness with the mother. It is to this Freud that we now turn our attention, the Freud of science, intellect, and reality, the Freud who views internal psychical space as a lesser reality.

■ THE FREUD OF SCIENCE, INTELLECT, AND REALITY ■

Freud's unique and original contribution to the study of the psychology of religion was his discovery that God is at times the psychical exaltation of the father of childhood. The insertion of, at times, is my doing, of course, since Freud was thoroughly convinced that God is an exalted father in every time and place. But is this really the case? God, to be sure, was at least a partial exaltation of Fiorella's father, but does this mean that God, or an individual's God-image, is always the bearer of residual traces of the Oedipus Complex? With the insertion of the phrase, at times, I have obviously betrayed my bias, a conviction I share with Rizzuto: God is at times at least a partial exaltation of the father of childhood, but not always. Here is where we must part ways with Freud and with a Freudian interpretation of religious faith, looking instead to the more contemporary neo-Freudian theorists of object relations, such as Rizzuto as well as to the theorist she builds her own work upon, namely, the British pediatrician and psychoanalyst, D. W. Winnicott. The genius of the object relations school has been to extend classical psychoanalytic theory beyond its embeddedness in oedipal theory, thus raising the possibility that everything psychical, including one's God-image, is not necessarily rooted in the Oedipus Complex.

Rizzuto directs our attention to the case of Douglas O'Duffy, which is representative of the second category of religious faith, or "category number two," made up of those individuals who want to believe in God if they could only be completely sure of God's existence. Douglas, a state police officer from Pennsylvania, was born and raised a Roman Catholic, and now, at age thirty-nine, still tries to take his religious faith very seriously. He is the youngest of ten children, born to Irish-American parents. What he told Rizzuto, during the course of his treatment for depression and obsessive-compulsive disorder, was that by the time his mother had given birth to her eighth child she no longer had anymore love left to give. Douglas, as far back as he can remember, brooded obsessively on the thought that it would have been better if he had never been born. With so many children living in the same household, there was little of mother to go around. Therefore, he harbored a deep bitterness and resentment toward his mother, because of her inability or unwillingness to give him the kind of love and attention he felt he deserved.

Conversely, Douglas looked up to his father with, to use Rizzuto's term, a *childish admiration* that precluded his seeing his father as a real person, possessing both strengths *and* limitations. However, in his early twenties, he learned, much to his disappointment, that his father was not infallible. It seems the father had been involved in a bribery scandal of shocking proportion, which Douglas did not learn of until just before his father's death. What this meant in very practical terms was that Douglas, unlike his older siblings, could not bring himself to move away from his hometown and follow his dream of getting a college education. For the next eight or nine years—up until his mother's death—Douglas's role would be the dutiful son, caring for his widowed mother. As he cared for her, he made it a point to try and engage her in "serious conversations," and to try and coax her into coming to live with him and his family. To say that she was unresponsive to his coaxing and cajoling would be, at least in Douglas's estimation, an understatement.

But this was not all Douglas wanted from his mother. More than anything else, he wanted, before she died, to have a corrective emotional experience. Borrowing conceptually from Freud's *The Interpretation of Dreams*, we could put it this way: the manifest or surface content is that Douglas wanted to have serious conversations with his mother and wanted her to come live with him and his family, but the manifest content only conceals from Douglas's own conscious awareness the deeper and unconscious latent content. And what might that latent content be? According to Rizzuto, Douglas wanted, from his mother, a corrective experience of responsive, rather than unresponsive mirroring. Recall that Douglas, even at age thirty-nine, had never begun working through his frustration and bitterness over his mother's preoccupation with the other siblings, and her apparent inability to recognize and appreciate him as a separate entity. To make matters worse, two of the siblings had died when they were babies, leaving the mother devastated and grief-stricken. The mother became so fixated on the second dead baby that when her new baby, Douglas, was born, she was either unable or unwilling to relate to him, unable or unwilling to give him the genuine mirroring a young child craves.

Douglas, then, was one of those babies who, in the words of Winnicott, "have a long experience of not getting back what they are giving." Winnicott, in *Playing and Reality*, continues this line of thought:

They look and do not see themselves. There are consequences. First, their own creative capacity begins to atrophy, and in some way or other they look around for other ways of getting something of themselves back from the environment. They may succeed by some other method, and blind infants need to get themselves reflected through other senses than that of sight. Indeed, a mother whose face is fixed may be able to respond in some other way. Most mothers can respond when the baby is in trouble or is aggressive, and especially when the baby is ill. Second, the baby gets settled in to the idea that when he or she looks, what is seen is the mother's face. The mother's face is not then a mirror. So perception takes the place of apperception, perception takes the place of that which might have been the beginning of a significant exchange with the world, a two-way process in which self-enhancement alternates with the discovery of meaning in the world of seen things.[22]

To paraphrase René Descartes, as a way of getting at this fundamental concept of object relations, because I am mirrored or seen by my primary caregiver, I am or I exist. Or, in the case of Douglas and other individuals who have a prolonged experience of not getting back, reciprocally, what they are giving, because I am not mirrored or seen by my primary caregiver, I am not or I do not exist, at least not in a meaningful or significant sort of way. In terms of the latter scenario, individuals who did not get their needs for mirroring met as young children will, according to Winnicott, spend the rest of their lives "painfully striving toward being seen, which is at the basis of creative looking." This is an exaggeration of the need we all share for mirroring, or an exaggeration of what is perfectly normal: "The exaggeration is the task of getting the mirror to notice and approve."[23] Indeed, this is precisely what Douglas was trying to accomplish, toward the end of his mother's life. The attempt to engage her in serious conversations and to coax her into coming to live with him was, at bottom, Douglas's way of giving his mother every opportunity to join him in a corrective emotional experience. On the surface or at the manifest-content level, it seems as if Douglas is simply being a dutiful son, yet, at the latent-content level of emotionality, he really wants, in the final days and months of his mother's life, the recognition and appreciation he has never fully received.

Now when it comes to Douglas's God-image, we might expect, if we take Freud as our guide, that it would resemble his father. Maybe, then, if we stay with our hunch, Douglas images his God as an admired Father, or, since his father's bribery scandal, as a Father with the power to do either good or evil. Douglas, after all, did tell Rizzuto that he was hesitant to fully believe in a God he was not sure existed, which may very well be indicative of a feeling of emotional ambivalence. And what is the root of emotional ambivalence? For Freud, it is nothing other than the Oedipus Complex, and the convoluted mixture of love and hate one feels toward one's father. If this is in fact the situation, then the case of Douglas is further confirmation of Freudian theory, that God is, psychologically, nothing other than an exalted father. Yet Rizzuto urges caution, and challenges us to resist the temptation to automatically situate Douglas within the oedipal mold of Freudian theory.

On the surface, Douglas does refer to God with the traditional language he has been given by the church, and does use masculine language and pronouns to refer to God. A closer psychodynamic look at the actual content of his description of God, however, suggests that his "God representation draws its characteristics mainly from the mother."[24] In other words, and this represents a radical departure from classical Freudian and psychoanalytic interpretation, Douglas's God-image is rooted, not in the oedipal experience of ages three to six, but even earlier, in the preoedipal years of infancy and very early childhood. If we put this in the language of classical psychoanalysis, and in the language of Freud's psychosexual theory of development, Douglas's God-image is rooted, not in the oedipal experience of the phallic stage, as Freud would have argued, but in the preoedipal experience of the oral and anal stages, sometime between birth and the age of three.

What, then, is the content of Douglas's God-image, which compels Rizzuto to deviate so resolutely from classical Freudian interpretation? Rizzuto asked Douglas, during the course of his treatment, to draw a picture of God. "While drawing, he explained, 'I know that God is there inside me—I don't know what it is. I have to find out inside me.' After he had completed the picture to his satisfaction, he wrote these cryptic words: 'I feel that God may be me in a mirror and that the only way I can open the Door is to know me completely and honestly.' "[25]

For Rizzuto, Douglas's choice of words could not be more striking: "I feel that God may be me in a *mirror*. . . ." Moreover, the ambiguity—God *may be* me in a mirror—is just as striking as the image of the mirror. Douglas seems to want more than anything to believe in God, if he could only be sure, ahead of time, of God's existence. However, without the fundamental certainty of God's existence, and of God's love and care, Douglas will not or cannot risk confessing and loving a God who may, when all is said and done, not respond to or return his love. Douglas, therefore, will not worship a God who may ignore his overtures of love, and will not "acknowledge the existence of a God who would pay no attention to him."[26] This happened once before to Douglas, in the preoedipal years of his life, and he is bound and determined to prevent it from happening again. All of this, suggests Rizzuto, harks back to the uneasy relation between Douglas and his mother, "one in which the child Douglas did not feel noticed as himself while he noticed his mother's capacity to respond to others (alive or dead) with affection and enthusiasm":

> I propose that this continued experience lent itself to the formation of a similar God representation, most specifically shown in the statement "I do not pray because I feel that God will not answer because he does not exist as I know him." What he seems to say is, "He does not exist for me the way I know he exists for others, from the way I see him behaving with them." Even more striking is the answer: "I think God is closest to those who believe and accept him (if you acknowledge God's existence)."[27]

In refusing to completely acknowledge or love a God who may *or* may not acknowledge or love him in return, Douglas, in a certain sense, is launching something of an intrapsychic preemptive strike whereby he can beat God to the proverbial punch, or, more precisely, beat God to the inevitable unresponsiveness or lack of recognition. Rizzuto, building on Winnicott, points out that this is a defensive maneuver, intended to protect the individual from experiencing the reactivation of the original pain and frustration vis-à-vis the primary caregiver. Douglas intuits that God will ultimately refuse to recognize and validate his existence, so he falls back upon that which is familiar, "a defensive maneuver of denying existence to the frustrating object." To put this more colloquially, he is really saying to God, "If you don't feel I exist I don't feel you exist either."[28]

Paradoxically, Douglas sees to it himself that his own children are grounded in the essential tenets of the Roman Catholic faith, because, in his mind, he does not want them to suffer through similar experiences of doubt and uncertainty. His children, though, must have experienced feelings of confusion and bewilderment, similar to the internal disconnect other children experience when their parents drop *them* off at church, on any given Sunday morning, and then proceed to drive to a favorite golf course or coffee shop. Douglas was basically saying to his children, "I want you to believe in God, even though I do not share this belief." More than likely, Douglas was living vicariously through his children, demanding that they acknowledge, with perfect assurance, the existence of God and thereby have with this God the satisfying relationship that he always wanted for himself. In any case, there was a double standard in the O'Duffy household: the children were to do as their father said, not as he did. While Douglas, no doubt, was painfully aware of this glaring incongruity, he was, in his present emotional and spiritual state, powerless to change it. As painful as the present incongruity happened to be, it was still not nearly as painful as facing the prospect that the God he might come to acknowledge and love could very well refuse to return his love.

What a situation like this would reactivate in Douglas, has reactivated in him, is the earlier frustration with his mother, when she would not or could not meet his need for mirroring. Consequently, he resorts to the defensive maneuver of keeping God at arm's length, of denying the existence of yet another object with the capacity to hurt and frustrate. We may, at this point, be asking ourselves the following question: Is there not a fundamental difference between the two objects—God and mother—and the way in which Douglas, or anyone for that matter, experiences them? While Douglas can, easily enough, deny the existence of a God that is *unseen*, this would seem to be more difficult with a maternal caregiver, who, for many years of his life, was very tangible and concrete. This, in fact, is the situation, which is why Douglas resorted to a *second* defensive maneuver, when it came to his mother. He obviously could not deny her actual existence, so what he did instead, psychically, was split her in two, into, on the one hand, an all-good mother and, on the other, an all-bad mother. Then he could, at least psychically, deny his mother's existence, or the image or representation of her as a caring and loving parent.

From Douglas's description of his mother, we might be inclined to surmise that she had little in the way of redeeming qualities. But to a psychoanalyst like Rizzuto, schooled in the discipline of psychodynamic interpretation, there is always more than meets the conscious eye, always more than what the client initially reports. When pressed, Douglas was able to be more objective, admitting to Rizzuto that his mother, while short on time, attention, and energy, still, in her own way, loved and cared for him. But with seven other children to love and care for, she could not give Douglas the individual attention, recognition, and mirroring that he seemed to desire. "One may conclude that it was not that the mother denied him care and warmth but that the child did not find in her the mirroring, the recognition he felt he needed in his own right." Rizzuto continues:

> In the case of Douglas O'Duffy the mother was represented as capable of perceiving others but not him—capable of warmth and enthusiasm but incapable of seeing anything in him to which she could respond with "accolades." The frustrated child seized that representation when in maturing it came time for him to elaborate his God representation. His frustration with his mother was never resolved. He hoped throughout his life to obtain the mirroring he did not obtain in childhood. He hoped that his extraordinary behavior and performance would cause his mother to notice him. But she failed him. That failure did not permit him to elaborate his God representation further and left it permanently linked with the frustrating mother. The care and good feeling also experienced in his relation with his mother were repressed in relation to her and to God as well.[29]

The case of Douglas, then, lends additional support to Freud's thesis: there is, at least to some extent, an intimate and inextricable psychical connection between the parental imagoes of childhood and one's image of God. As it was with Fiorella, the parental imagoes of Douglas exerted a lasting influence, in a sense setting the boundaries for how he was to image God. Because the psychical representations of one's parents are *zeitlos*, "timeless" and therefore indestructible, there will never come a day, for Douglas, Fiorella, or for anyone else, when parental imagoes and images of God are entirely disentangled. Douglas's God-image, so intimately connected to, and associated with, the psychical representation of his mother, had, paraphrasing Freud's words in *Moses and Monotheism*, a compulsive character: it *must* be believed. Freud, of course, would have had no problem supporting the view that Douglas's God-image had a compulsive character. What he would not have supported, in any way, shape, or form, was Rizzuto's conclusion that Douglas's God-image drew its characteristics mainly from the mother, or from the mother representation. Recall how testy Freud had gotten when his friend, Romain Rolland, had the audacity to disagree with him over the origin of the need for religion, locating it, not in the oedipal period of development, but earlier, in the oceanic feeling of oneness with the mother.

Locating the origin of the need for religion in the oceanic feeling of oneness with the mother corresponds to locating it, as Rizzuto does with the case of Douglas, in the preoedipal years of development. Rizzuto, at this point, would be closer to Rolland than to Freud. What is refreshing about Rizzuto's work is her willingness to hold opposing views in tension, finding, at certain times, Freudian theory to have unique explanatory power, while, at other times, exchanging the oedipal interpretation of Freudian theory for the preoedipal interpretation of object relations theory. The clinician, as she has so deftly demonstrated, must have multiple theories at his or her disposal, applying, with a client like Fiorella, Freud's interpretation of religion, or, with a client like Douglas, an interpretation informed by object relations theory. While Fiorella's need for religion seems in fact to be rooted in the oedipal stage of development, the same cannot be said for the religious faith of Douglas. Fiorella, on the one hand, longs for the continuity of protection and consolation, so characteristic of the oedipal years, while Douglas, on the other hand, longs for a corrective experience of genuine mirroring, more characteristic of the preoedipal years.

Freud, it is fair to say, had a one-track mind when it came to the interpretation of religious faith as psychological projection. What the religious believer is projecting, in every conceivable time and place, is the image of the oedipal father. This may be true, to some extent, for individuals like Fiorella, but it is hardly an adequate interpretation for individuals like Douglas. In terms of the latter, the interpretation offered us by Rizzuto and Rolland is much more persuasive: what the individual is projecting is the image of the mother, and what the individual is longing for, at least in part, is the original state or feeling of oneness with her. But what if, as in the case of Douglas, there never was a state of original oneness with the mother—actual or perceived? What then? How might Douglas work his way through this emotional and spiritual impasse, through the feelings of anger, bitterness, hurt, and disappointment he harbors toward his God and mother, since the two are intimately linked together in his psyche? How might any religious believer—Douglas, Fiorella, you, or I—begin letting go of an underdeveloped and not altogether healthy God-image that was formed in response to a particular situation in childhood, but now, in adulthood, is in dire need of being reimaged and transformed?

At this point, we cannot look to Freud, unless, of course, we wish to settle for a purely reductive solution. The Freud of science, intellect, and *material* reality will urge us to abandon our childish and illusory pursuits, in hopes of getting us to resign ourselves to the impersonal or depersonified world of Ananke or "harsh necessity." In other words, human beings must be willing to adapt themselves to the way things are "out there" in the external world of material reality. To talk of reimaging and transforming reality "in here," inside the psyche, would have been interpreted by Freud as purely narcissistic. The real world is "out there," in the realm of external objects. And since, as Freud believed, God does not exist out there in external reality, it is an utter waste of time and valuable human energy to be talking about the reimaging or the transformation of one's God-image within the realm of psychical space. We human beings, therefore, must accept reality *as it is*, and stop deceiving ourselves that it could be anything else. Give up the childish idea of God, Freud seems to be saying; stop regressing, emotionally, to the early years of childhood, and start becoming a mature adult.

Yet, is illusionless or projectionless adulthood the highest ideal for human beings? If you are Freud, a product of Enlightenment thinking, and a champion of the scientific method, the answer can only be a resounding, "yes!" Like Rizzuto, however, we must disagree with Freud, but not totally. Human beings do, at times, empty too much of themselves into the heavens, or, like Fiorella and Douglas, expend too much of their vitality and creativity on God-images that do not further their emotional and spiritual development. What, then, might the solution be, for Fiorella and Douglas? And what might the solution or the goal be for others of us, who have come to discover that updating and reimaging and transforming one's image of God is ultimately a lifelong process, something that must be addressed at every stage of the life cycle?

For Freud, the issue of whether one is in possession of an underdeveloped God-image or one that is more developed and life-enhancing is utterly moot. Since God is nothing more than an exalted father, nothing more than the product of a highly fragile and vulnerable psyche, God can only be a psychological crutch that retards our intellectual growth and development. Believers who think of themselves as more progressive, or feel they are in possession of an updated and transformed God-image, are simply fooling themselves, for religious faith in any and every shape and form is always the product of an immature and neurotic psyche. The equation, for Freud, can only be either-or: either human beings, aided by science, grow up into reality and accept it for what it is—devoid of any divinity—or they devote their lives to believing in and serving a God who, regrettably, is only satisfied with their acquiescence and subservience.

But might there not be some sort of middle ground between these two extremes, another alternative besides either resigning ourselves to the harsh and cold reality of Ananke or remaining, psychologically, children forever, in the service of a God or God-image formed in the earliest years of life? Freud would say, "no," primarily because of his overvaluation of material reality and his undervaluation or devaluation of psychical space. This, to be very clear, is where we must necessarily part ways with Freud, looking instead to object relations theorists, like Rizzuto and Winnicott, especially if we intend to be of help to individuals like Fiorella and Douglas. As Rizzuto observes, "Freud's solution for himself was a stark and stoic realism with no consolation but the pride of being able to accept suffering and terror without clinging to anyone." Others, he believed, should follow suit by imitating his courageous example:

> Freud claimed that human beings must be stoical, renouncing their wishes for protection and consolation. They must stop cling-ing to their fathers and to God, his substitute. The best they can and must do is to face their fate and believe in science; that will make them true adults. The analyst, however, must ask why it is that clinging to the father, in whatever form, has become for Freud synonymous with infantile wishes. Is it possible to cling to a father as an adult; is there such a thing as mature clinging?[30]

■ THE IMPORTANCE OF PSYCHICAL REALITY ■

One cannot underestimate the importance of Rizzuto's question, Is there such a thing as mature clinging or healthy attachment, to either a father or mother, as well as to God? True, Fiorella and Douglas, at least presently, do seem to exemplify an immature and unhealthy clinging to psychical images of parents and God, but might there not come a day when, after they have begun working through their painful feelings, they forge a more mature attachment to updated and transformed images of parents and God? The disciplines of pastoral counseling, spiritual direction, and psychotherapy dem-onstrate, again and again, that it is certainly possible to reimage and trans-form our underdeveloped or misdeveloped images of others and God.

What is important to keep in mind is that individuals like Fiorella and Douglas have a third option, one that would lead them beyond either the dogmatism of Freudian theory or that of traditional religion. On the one hand, if Fiorella and Douglas embrace the conventional wisdom of Freudian interpretation, they will renounce all ties to psychical images of God, with-out any further discussion. On the other hand, if they listen to the conven-tional wisdom of traditional Christian theology, they will need to abide by the external images of God presented to them by the church, without, again,

any further discussion. At present, there are only two options: either renounce and be done with God, and grow up into reality, or be faithful to the
God of one's father and mother and remain, as Freud so pejoratively put it,
a child forever. But in the context of pastoral counseling, spiritual direction,
or spiritually attentive psychotherapy, it is in fact possible for someone to do
both: confess, love, and trust God while growing up into reality. This is the
third and by far the healthier and more integrative option. The first two
options—either renounce the God who has frustrated or disappointed us, or
swear allegiance, unquestioningly and unhesitatingly, to the God we inherited from our youth—can only leave us fragmented and psychically split,
unable to integrate the past with the present.

Renouncing a disappointing God and confessing, unreflectively, the
God handed us by our parents or church are, in a sense, two variations on
the same theme or dynamic. In both cases, the individual fears having to
confront the hurt, pain, frustration, and disappointment associated with parental imagoes and images of God. This, as Rizzuto has convincingly demonstrated in her recent book, *Why Did Freud Reject God?* was exactly what
Freud wanted to avoid facing within himself: the pain associated with images
of parents and God. Freud, then, had his conscious, theoretical reasons for
not believing in God, *as well as* his unconscious, emotional ones. Rizzuto's
archaeology of Freud's life and psyche poses a serious challenge to his cherished belief that renouncing or denying the existence of God always represents a move toward health and maturity. In fact, her work serves to illustrate
that Freud, in certain ways, was also destined to remain, emotionally and
spiritually, a child forever. I will have more to say about this shortly.

The alternative is to find a more creative and integrative solution, a
healthy middle ground between the two extremes of renouncing a disappointing God and an unreflective religious faith. Freud, it is fair to say, can be of
little help here, for the human individual, according to Freudian theory, must
make a choice between one of two extremes: either embrace religious faith and
remain a child forever, or give up the security blanket of God and religion and
courageously accept the travails and disappointments of human living, without
clinging to any external or internal means of support. In other words, Freud
offers Fiorella and Douglas nothing of a creative solution, but only a stark and
stoic realism with little or no hope or consolation. Freud, as we have already
noted, made a point to steer clear of the prophetic role, explaining that he has
nothing hopeful to offer the human individual. This is hardly surprising, since
religious faith and devotion to God, in Freudian theory, is little more than a
regressive psychical attachment to the primary caregivers of early childhood.

But what if God is more than that? What if, in the case of Fiorella and Douglas, God has the potential of becoming, psychically and spiritually, more than God has ever been before?

This, as Ricoeur pointed out in chapter 2, is the teleological dimension of religious faith, something that Freud could not or would not see. Rizzuto, in responding to this Freudian interpretation of religion, states rather un-equivocally that human life is diminished and impoverished when our im-ages of God "vanish under the repression of a psychic realism that does violence to the ceaseless creativity of the human mind."[31] This, it must be understood, is the key and principle ingredient missing from a Freudian interpretation of religious faith: the capacity to creatively update and trans-form our images of God, which, in turn, will influence the way in which we image ourselves and others. Freud, in offering us little more than a Sisyphean resignation to Fate or reality *as it is*, is simply unable to lead us out of the painful and fatalistic morass of an either-or determinism.

We should not, however, be surprised at this finding, for a theory that discounts psychical space as a lesser reality will discern little value in the creative reimaging and transformation of internal images and representa-tions. That is why we must turn away from Freud, looking instead to object relations theorists, like Rizzuto and Winnicott, who value psychical space as real and meaningful in its own right, since it is the realm where human beings make sense of their experience. For example, if Fiorella and Douglas are to find a new and creative way of living, they will need to do more than simply accept Ananke or harsh reality, for what it is. They will also need to probe the depths of their internal reality, updating and transforming, again and again, their God-image in order to keep it up-to-date with their "epige-netically and historically changing personality."[32]

All of this presupposes yet another reality, one that we could almost describe as an intermediate reality, a realm or region located somewhere between subjectivity and objectivity, between the worlds of material and psychical reality. Object relations theorists refer to this third dimension of reality as the "transitional space," or intermediate area of experience, which does not come exclusively from either the inner psychical world of subjec-tivity or the external world of objectivity. According to Winnicott, it comes from both:

> My claim is that if there is a need for this double statement, there is also a need for a triple one: the third part of the life of a human being, a part that we cannot ignore, is an intermediate

area of *experiencing,* to which inner reality and external life contribute. It is an area that is not challenged, because no claim is made on its behalf except that it shall exist as a resting-place for the individual engaged in the perpetual human task of keeping inner and outer reality separate yet interrelated.[33]

In many ways, this intermediate area of experience, or transitional space, corresponds to Erik Erikson's discovery of "an intermediate reality between phantasy and actuality," which becomes, for the individual, "an indispensable harbor for the overhauling of shattered emotions after periods of rough going in the social seas."[34] Sadly, though, it is almost as if Fiorella and Douglas have no transitional space or intermediate area of repose, to which they may go for the overhauling of shattered emotions, as well as for the overhauling of their stunted God-image. This lack of a sufficiently developed transitional space or intermediate area is primarily what brought Fiorella and Douglas to Rizzuto in the first place. At present, they simply do not have, in their possession, the requisite internal resources needed to reimage and reelaborate their underdeveloped representation of God. Nor can Freud be much of a resource, since we can almost hear him telling them to "get over" their childish wishes and illusions, to instead face the real world of external reality. And yet, much of the emotional pain that Fiorella and Douglas are presently experiencing has less to do with facing external reality and more to do with their inability to face and subsequently update and transform the objects and images of internal psychical space.

Taking a rather subtle shot at Freud and at classical psychoanalysis, Winnicott reminds us that "you may cure your patient and not know what it is that makes him or her go on living. It is of first importance for us to acknowledge openly that absence of psychoneurotic illness may be health, but it is not life."[35] Or, to paraphrase Winnicott, it is of first importance for us to acknowledge that the absence of the psychoneurotic illness of religious faith, or the renunciation of all attachment to our images of God, may seem like health to the analyst but may not be life-giving to the client. This is undoubtedly why Rizzuto keeps her distance from the Freudian prescription for psychological health, which makes the renunciation of attachment to parents and God a prerequisite to health, in every time and place. She urges her clients, like Fiorella and Douglas, to refrain from abandoning their images of God. Instead, her clients are encouraged to exchange their underdeveloped images for those that promote growth, healing, and transformation.

Thus, Rizzuto seems to have answered her own question: yes, there is such a thing as mature and healthy attachment.

But if Rizzuto teaches us anything with her clinical data, it is that mature attachment to God comes only *after* one has revised and transformed the God-image of one's childhood and youth. We may therefore deduce from Rizzuto's work that God is, psychically and spiritually, either a source of splitting or fragmentation—as we have seen with Fiorella and Douglas—or an integrative force for renewal and change. The latter, the integrative dimension of God, and the fact that God may indeed be something more than an exalted father, ultimately takes us beyond the reductionism of Freudian theory. Attachment to God is not necessarily an indication of a neurotic or immature psyche, as Freud believed. It could be, but it could also be indicative of a healthy and integrated psyche, and of a transitional space or intermediate area of experience that is still very much alive and well. "People's dealings with their God," writes Rizzuto, in her essay, "Object Relations and the Formation of the Image of God," "are no more, and no less complex than their dealings with other people—either in early childhood or in any other age; i.e. they are imperfect, ambiguous, dynamic and, by their very nature, have potential for both integrating and fragmenting their overall psychic experience."[36]

Religious faith, from what we have learned, may in fact represent something more than a regressive and immature attachment to the psychical images and representations of childhood, and the subsequent projection of these unaltered images into the divine sphere. True, as we saw with Ricoeur, religious faith will always, to some extent, be the bearer of residual traces of primitive and regressive immaturity. Human beings, individually and collectively, have a very deep longing to return to an Edenic state of innocence, to that original consolatory state with a protective father and/or the original oneness with a nurturing mother. The Christian confession of original sin, and the fact that human beings have supposedly fallen from an original state of bliss and grace, would seem to support the link between regressive immaturity and religious faith. Still, religious faith has the potential to offer something more than a regression to primitive immaturity. This is the teleological dimension of religion, something that Freud, in the midst of his one-sided and reductive interpretation, could not or would not see. Religious faith, then, not only puts us back in touch, regressively, with the original feelings and impressions of childhood, but also points us forward in the quest for new and reimagined meaning.

Nor can the regressive dimension of religious faith, in and of itself, be automatically and pejoratively construed as the neurotic side of the equation. Earlier, Rizzuto asked if there might be such a thing as healthy and mature clinging or attachment. In the same vein, it would be worth our while to ask a similar question, Is there such a thing as healthy regression? Or does regression always represent an unhealthy escape from reality, an unconscious flight back to early primitive experience, in order to avoid dealing with the present and the future? Sometimes, but not always. It is important to keep in mind that the psychical destination to which the individual is regressing may in fact be the transitional space or intermediate area of experience. If this is the case, then the individual's regressive maneuver may actually serve an integrative purpose, by serving to enliven and reenergize his or her personal world. To put all of this in the context of religious faith, we may say that contrary to Freud's view that the believer is merely escaping into a psychical world of unreality, the believer may actually be regressing to the transitional space—that is, the birthplace of creativity, imagination, and reimagination—in order to contemporize and revitalize his or her God-image.

Rizzuto has no problem admitting that "God, psychologically speaking, is an illusory transitional object," as long as we remember that God is a unique and special type of transitional object, "because unlike teddy bears, dolls, or blankets made out of plushy fabrics, [God] is created from representational material whose sources are the representations of primary objects."[37] Since God can never, as a representational object, be tossed into some toy chest, and, along with the teddy bear, doll, and blanket, be completely forgotten, God has the capacity to remain "a potentially available representation for the continuous process of psychic integration."[38] God, it should be added, remains a potentially available representation for the duration of a person's life. However, we must not lose sight of the double-edged nature of one's psychical image of God: it has the capacity to either be a source of fragmentation and splitting or a source of integration and wholeness.

In Freud's view, there is only room for two realities: subjective reality and objective reality. It would take the object relations school, and theorists like Rizzuto and Winnicott, to amend Freudian theory, adding, so to speak, the missing piece to the unfinished puzzle: the transitional space or intermediate area of experience. This third reality, which exists in between internality and externality, is where religious believers cannot help but go, regressively, if they intend to transform a personal God-image into a contemporary and relevant source of integration and inspiration. Rizzuto admits that "in evaluating Freud's work, I first agreed with his premise":

> The God of everyday man could not just be a rational idea but the representational creation of a living being, originating in the child's experiences with those who interacted with him at the

beginning of life. I also disagree with Freud. If God had such origins, the significance for human life, particularly for the meaning of a person's life, must be more than a regressive attachment to the parents of childhood. In fact, the God representation *must have the same ceaseless potential for new meanings in the long process of life as the parental representations have for us until we die.* Further, both the father *and* the mother provide the experiences for a later formation of a God representation.[39]

But, as Rizzuto has clearly demonstrated in *Why Did Freud Reject God?* it could not have been otherwise for Freud. It is remarkable that what Freud deemed the essence of the need for religion, namely, the longing for protection and consolation, was precisely what formed the essence of his unbelief. The biographical record indicates that what was missing from Freud's early life—something that he never came to terms with, consciously or unconsciously—was the fact that he never felt protected and consoled as a child. The young Freud found it more than a little distressing to learn of his father's humiliation at the hands of certain townspeople. Even more disturbing was his father's apparent indifference and impotence, in the face of such disgrace. To be sure, Freud would never, from this moment on, feel *protected* by such a weak and ineffective father. Nor could he turn to his mother for any *consolation*, for she would insist that he follow her example of responding to adversity and suffering with stoic resignation. Unfortunately, Freud's parental imagoes or representations would not have the ceaseless potential for new meanings, primarily because he never came to terms with the pain and disappointment associated with them. It is rather ironic that the psychoanalyst par excellence, who spent most of his working life encouraging patients to face and work through the frustrations and traumas of their early years, would himself stay as far away as he could from his own personal emotional pain.

How was Freud, who at one point had subjected himself to a period of intense self-scrutiny and self-analysis, so successful in keeping the emotional pain associated with his early years at arm's length? Rizzuto could not be any clearer: Freud took his frustration and disappointment out on a "safer" target: God and religion. She wants us to see that it is hardly coincidental that Freud had the greatest difficulty understanding the religious believer's longing for protection and consolation from a benevolent Providence, since this is what he himself never received as a child. Thus, Freud, with his critique of religion, seems to be saying to the religious believer: how dare you presume to be protected and consoled by a heavenly Parent, when some of us have yet to receive any protection and consolation from our earthly parents. Rizzuto refers to this as "the rage of [Freud's] loneliness."[40] According to Rizzuto, the "evidence" for this rage of loneliness comes from Freud's preoccupation or obsession with the origin of religious faith. This is the supreme paradox, and it is most illustrative of Freud's internal conflict over the issue: while dismissing religious faith as, at best, something irrelevant or, at worst, as something deleterious to the human species, he could not keep himself from thinking and writing about it.

Freud, therefore, who prided himself on being, first and foremost, the champion of science and reason, was not that different from the religious believer. He, too, was projecting his internal world of object relations into the divine realm, albeit negatively. "Freud's personal suffering," Rizzuto suggests, "had become articulated in his theory about religion for all humankind"; he would make God "pay in displacement for the failure of all his primary objects."[41] Said another way, Freud, the unreconstructed nineteenth-century gentleman, said to God what he was afraid to say to his parents, either in person or in fantasy. He could not, much like Douglas, entrust himself to the care of a benevolent Providence, for this, coming on the heels of painful childhood experiences, would have been a recipe for further disappointment and frustration. As Rizzuto observes, Freud's contempt for the feeble religious faith of human beings "sounds like a muffled complaint about his family. . . . He never complained overtly about his parents, but the forcefulness of his sentences hints at suppressed suffering and rage displaced onto God and the absence of protection."[42]

■ F O U R ■

The Relation Between Religious and Gender Psychology

> Ambiguity is not only a way of knowing the sacred but also a quality of
> sacredness itself, as we experience, for example, in the awe-fulness of
> birthing and dying. It is, on the one hand, assurance of redemptive
> possibility in all moments of life. On the other hand, it frustrates the
> search for any one truth, any one way.
>
> Kathleen Greider, *Reckoning with Aggression*

The final theorist, Judith Van Herik, working in the field of feminist
theory, is convinced that because Freud and Freudianism have been so
influential in the West, it is important for us to continue to return to
Freud's writings. She urges her feminist colleagues, as well as the religious
community, to resist the temptation to write off Freud because he came to
certain disagreeable and offensive conclusions about the nature of femininity
and the nature of religious faith. On the surface, this sounds as if Van Herik
is headed in a direction similar to that of Paul Ricoeur and Ana-Maria Rizzuto:
those of us living in the West must be in conversation with Freud, because of
his extraordinary influence. A closer look, however, indicates that she is headed,
methodologically, in a completely different direction from the two previous
theorists, a direction that is less normative vis-à-vis Freud and more theoretically neutral.

At the beginning of *Freud on Femininity and Faith*, Van Herik informs
us that she does not intend to take any position—pro or con—toward Freud
and psychoanalysis, or toward a Freudian interpretation of femininity and
religion. She states, for example, that "I find Freud's thought intellectually
valuable; my concern is with its challenges when read as a theory of culture
more than with its clinical utility."[1] Van Herik, in other words, finds Freud's
work on religion and gender intellectually valuable because it gives us important clues about contemporary religio-cultural attitudes in the West, attitudes that are harbored both in the individual and in the collective psyche.

As for the clinical and hermeneutical utility of Freudian theory, Van Herik appears less interested. "The intention of this interpretation," she writes, "is to show how diverse parts of Freud's writings fit together into a message about the related inner meanings of patricentric culture, psychological gender, and religious belief." Her "primary interest, then, is not in what is correct or incorrect in Freud's views of femininity and masculinity but in the critical weight these views have."[2] This methodological stance, applied to Freud's view of masculinity and femininity, will also, as we will see, be applied to Freud's view of religious faith as psychological projection.

■ MASCULINITY AND THE REALITY PRINCIPLE ■

Van Herik engages Freud for reasons other than trying to learn what Freud can teach us about the human individual's willingness to tolerate moral condemnation from a punishing Deity in exchange for the promise of eternal consolation and protection (Ricoeur's goal) or about the psychical representation or image of God and its relation to parental imagoes (Rizzuto's goal). In contrast to both Ricoeur and Rizzuto, she does not set out to prove or disprove the clinical or hermeneutical utility of Freudian theory. Rather, Van Herik is more interested in the connection between Freud's pejorative view of religious faith as mere psychological projection and his asymmetrical theory of gender. In fact, as she will argue, we cannot fully understand Freud's view of religion apart from a thoroughgoing understanding of his views on masculinity and femininity, and vice versa. Therefore, instead of attempting to ascertain the clinical or hermeneutical utility of Freudian theory, or the lack thereof, Van Herik's goal is to determine the critical weight of Freud's views on gender and religion within the context of Western culture.

She realizes, and rightly so, that she, a feminist theorist, will be dealing with a subject that, to state the obvious, is rather controversial. The feminist jury, so to speak, is still out on the subject of Freud, and whether or not women are obligated to converse with him and his theory. Indeed, as Philip Rieff has stated, Freud's misogyny *is* more than prejudice; it is a vital intellectual function in his system. Van Herik points out, in her essay, "The Feminist Critique of Classical Psychoanalysis," that feminist questions have been asked of "the whole of Freud's psychoanalytic corpus, about its complex and variously interpreted messages about human nature and culture." She continues:

On the one hand, Freudian theory as a whole has been seen as an influential example of sexist theory, so that Freud is taken as an important contemporary enforcer of sexism. On the other hand, in a move that some may consider paradoxical, the Freudian texts have been understood as a resource for feminist analysis, as material with which to design a feminist remedy for sexist culture as a whole. Those who see Freud as prototypical sexist ask: what are the defining characteristics of sexist theory? And where are these characteristics found in Freud's writings? Here, everything which assays his mind, including his letters and personal life, is relevant data. Those who want to use Freudian theory for feminist construction ask: how does Freudian psychoanalytic theory account for systematic, apparently universal sexism? How is this account useful for a feminist analysis of the problem? And, what programme for change does this analysis suggest? Here, data is not his personal views or conduct, but the logic of his theory.[3]

Van Herik refrains from taking sides, by not telling us explicitly which of the two feminist views she supports. Freudian theory, though, by its very nature, refuses to let us take a completely neutral stance. Consequently, Van Herik would have strengthened an already-persuasive and well-developed argument, if she had simply located herself, methodologically, within one of these two feminist approaches to Freud: either the first of the two feminist views, which bars Freud and his theory from any meaningful discussion of gender because of its overt sexism, or the second view, which tends to include Freud in the discussion on gender because, despite his sexist and misogynistic tone, he still has much to teach us about the patricentric predicament of Western culture. The first view sees Freud as having created a theory *of* gender, while the second view sees Freud as having created a theory *about* gender situated in a patriarchal context.[4]

We could obviously infer that Van Herik has located herself within the latter framework, since her neutrality toward Freud would seem to suggest, at least to some extent, a certain degree of open-mindedness. To be sure, it hardly seems likely that she would write off Freud as a result of his sexist and misogynistic views, agreeing with Mary Daly that Freudian theory is a "religion" of patriarchy, the "hideous blossom" of the Judeo-Christian tradition.[5] Still, it would help to hear from Van Herik herself that this is in fact her stance toward psychoanalysis. This, again, would serve to further strengthen an approach to Freud that is already persuasive and compelling.

Van Herik, in her analysis of Freudian theory, makes an important discovery: masculinity, for Freud, "because of its special relationships to paternity, becomes normative, objective, universal, and more valuable than femininity . . . it expresses the victory of mind over sense."[6] Certainly, in Freudian theory, the boundary between masculinity in particular and humanity in general is blurred; the two—the masculine and the human—are essentially one and the same. This, argues Van Herik, is primarily due to the fact that for Freud, masculinity is the universal norm or standard while femininity can best be described as a deviation or departure from the standard, an exception to the norm. Thus, when Freud speaks of *human* development, he has in mind, first and foremost, the development of the *male* individual.

To put this in the context of Freud's own native tongue, we could state that when he said *Mensch,* or "human being," he meant *Mann,* or "man." And, if those of us in the Western world have in fact internalized so much of Freud's theory, as Ricoeur, Rizzuto, and now Van Herik all believe, then what happens is that we, too, like Freud, mean *Mann* when we say or think *Mensch.* Less often do we as a culture conceptualize femininity as the norm, the standard by which we compare masculinity; it is usually the other way around. Nor are the two—masculinity and femininity—even close to being on equal footing. "In asymmetrical theory," writes Van Herik, "as soon as the human norm and the human subject are assimilated to the masculine, the image of the human ideal easily becomes masculine."[7]

But, as we have observed elsewhere in this book, maybe this is simply indicative of Freud being a product of his time, a time when society as a whole would have assimilated the human to the masculine. Maybe now, alas, we can, along with Peter Gay, attribute Freud's gender asymmetry to the fact that he was an unreconstructed nineteenth-century gentleman, never quite adjusting his old-fashioned manners to a new age with more progressive ideas about women. On the surface, this certainly seems like an adequate and plausible explanation, until we pause with Van Herik to explore, in greater detail, the issue of gender asymmetry in Freudian theory. Is Freud merely an unreconstructed gentleman, a theorist whose formulations and ideas simply reflect the "natural standpoint" of his time and place? Or, did Freud have other reasons—personal and professional—for assimilating the *Mensch* to the *Mann,* the human to the masculine?

Van Herik calls our attention to the "critical principle" of Freudian theory, the normative and definitive standard that guided and informed Freud's study of development, gender, and religious faith: the renunciation of illusion. In terms of human, or male development, we have seen this in the young boy's renunciation of the illusion that he can possess his mother and do away with his father, at the conclusion of the Oedipus Complex. After all, what choice does he have, when the threat of castration is in the air? The young girl, on the other hand, since she never has to fear the threat of castration, does not have to renounce the illusion of attachment to the parents with the same force and intensity as that of the boy. According to Freud, the renunciation of illusion is manifested most powerfully in the scientific spirit, which heroically resists the temptation to look for an imaginary benevolent Providence in the context of religious faith.

Freud, as noted, defined illusions, not as errors, but as the fulfillments of the oldest, strongest, and most urgent wishes of humanity. Moreover, Freud suggests that "we call a belief an illusion when a wish-fulfillment is a prominent factor in its motivation, and in doing so we disregard its relation to reality, just as the illusion itself sets no store by verification."[8] The fundamental problem, as far as Freud was concerned, and the reason why he sharply disagreed with the rhetorical opponent in *The Future of an Illusion*, is that an illusion, in any shape or form, represents a formidable obstacle to the intellectual and cultural advancement of the human species. What, then, is the alternative? In a word, *renunciation*. And, according to Van Herik, "the paradigmatic renunciation, in Freud's view, is the son's renunciation of oedipal libido,"[9] the healthy exchange of the pleasure principle for the reality principle.

The young girl, as we discovered in chapter 1, does not share the same sense of urgency, in terms of the renunciation of oedipal libido. In contrast to the boy, she can enjoy the libidinal attachment to her parents for as long as she likes, and the accompanying illusion that her parents will always be there for her, at least intrapsychically, to comfort, console, and protect her. At this point, we can begin to see the connections Van Herik will be making, when she compares Freud's psychology of gender to his psychology of religion. She writes:

> Freud's critical themes of wish fulfillment, illusion, and instinctual renunciation guide his psychoanalytic studies of religion and correspond to his evaluative understandings of femininity and masculinity as asymmetrical in structure. ("Evaluative" means simply that Freud considers masculinity and femininity to be of uneven value both as psychical attitudes and as positions in culture). But Freud did not deliberately look at religion through

the categorical lenses that he developed in his studies of mascu-linity and femininity. Rather, the relationship between gender and religion is mediated by his critical themes of illusion and renunciation. Renunciation *of* illusion is Freud's consistent criti-cal principle; it grounds both his critique of femininity within the theory of gender and of illusion within the theory of religion. In these terms, the specific values which Freud awards masculinity measure the valuable in general. The specific failures in value which he attributes to femininity measure such failure in general.[10]

What, exactly, are the specific values that Freud awards to masculinity? And what are the specific failures in value that he attributes to femininity? Let us, for the time being, stay with the "more valuable" masculinity, before we begin exploring the "less valuable" femininity, and the parallels between the latter and devotion to religious faith. We have already highlighted the most fundamental and highly prized value of all, which Freud awards exclu-sively to masculinity, namely, the renunciation of oedipal libido. Recall that the young boy, who would like nothing more than to wrest his mother away from his father, realizes that he does not stand a chance against the bigger and more powerful father. As a result, he abandons the libidinal—that is, sexual—cathexis to his mother, as well as the libidinal—that is, aggressive—cathexis to his father. But there is more. The boy, in exchanging primary pleasure for secondary pleasure, or, in exchanging the pleasure principle for the reality principle, begins to intuit that he has adopted an attitude toward his father that is not very different from his mother's attitude toward her husband.

Although the boy cannot consciously put his feelings into words, he is still, at an unconscious level, particularly sensitive to the fact that he now shares with his mother a passive feminine attitude toward the father. Thus, what we witness in the young boy is the birth of, to use the Adlerian term, the *masculine protest* against passivity, dependence, and submission, or, in a word, *femininity*. To feel more powerful and less vulnerable, or, to feel more masculine and less feminine, the boy proceeds to introject and identify with the values and standards of his father, and, in so doing, *renounces* the original libidinal attachment to his earliest caregivers. As Freud theorized in "Some Psychical Consequences of the Anatomical Distinction Between the Sexes," the Oedipus Complex is not merely dissolved. Instead, because of the shock of threatened castration, it is literally "smashed to pieces."

What emerges is the normative standard by which human develop-ment is measured in the Western world: separation, independence, and a renunciation of feminine attachment to the psychical images of mother and father. Assuming the role of devil's advocate, one may feel inclined to ask, "But is the boy's identification with the father, and the introjection of paternal values and standards, not a form of attachment to the psychical representation of the father?" At first glance, this appears to be the case, until we stop to recall that the introjection of paternal values is something of a *secondary* attachment, since the more primary and pleasurable attachments have already, under the threat of castration, been abandoned. It is nothing short of the triumph of culture over the individual, the triumph of reality over primary pleasure, and, even more significant, the triumph of masculine detachment over feminine attachment. "The dissolution of the Oedipus Complex," writes Van Herik, "is the paradigmatic Freudian renunciation; if it is truly a dissolution, the way is prepared for the masculine and the psychological ideal of independence from parents (especially from ambivalent defiance of and submission to the father) and activity in the world."[11]

Nancy Chodorow, in *The Reproduction of Mothering*, makes the same connection as Van Herik: in Western culture, masculinity goes hand in hand with independence and separation, whereas femininity goes hand in hand with attachment and relationality. Chodorow points out that while feminine identification processes are primarily relational, masculine identification processes "stress differentiation from others, the denial of affective relation, and categorical universalistic components of the masculine role." In short, "masculine identification processes tend to deny relationship,"[12] or the importance of attachment. Moreover, in a patriarchal culture, which has yet to forge a lasting egalitarianism between the sexes, masculine renunciation of attachment becomes the prototypical standard, the norm to which we aspire as a culture, while feminine attachment becomes a deviation from the norm. Van Herik, building on Chodorow, makes a similar observation, which prepares the way for her application of Freud's psychology of gender to his psychology of religion:

> Renunciation explains mental, masculine, and cultural development. Analogously, renunciation is the principle by which the individual is cured of unwitting bondage to passions and by which culture is cured of unwitting bondage to religious illusion. When renunciation is the source of higher development toward reality and independence, the psychical modes achieved by renunciation criticize those psychical modes which have been renounced. Just as renunciation overcomes illusion, paternity overcomes

maternity, masculinity overcomes femininity, reality overcomes wish, and science overcomes religion. In each case, the former term is the source of judgment on the latter; it is the criterion by which the latter term is diagnosed as regressive, narcissistic, wishful.[13]

Through masculinity's obedience to the reality principle, in the form of the renunciation of feminine attachment to archaic objects—for instance, psychical images of mother and father—and to archaic desires and wishes—for instance, the illusion that one can find eternal love and protection from an earthly and/or heavenly parent—the way has been opened for human beings to move forward, in terms of the intellectual and cultural evolution of the species. This, quite naturally, is Freud's prescription for the advancement of the species: the renunciation of psychical attachment to archaic objects. Van Herik refers to this as the Freudian theory of "ideal masculinity," the goal to which human beings, individually and collectively, must strive if they are to ever extricate themselves from their present state of infantilization. Obviously, the implication is that the Western world, as a whole, still has a ways to go before it can call itself an "enlightened culture," which can only mean that it has yet to transform the present standard of "normal masculinity" into the more advanced standard of ideal masculinity.

Part of, or actually much of the problem has to do with the way in which the modern individual dissolves the Oedipus Complex. Remember, for example, that Freud held that the young boy does not simply dissolve the Oedipus Complex, but rather, under the ominous cloud of threatened castration, feels compelled to smash it to pieces by abandoning his wish to possess the mother and to do away with the father. The boy hurriedly introjects the values of the father into the ego, "where they form the nucleus of the super-ego and give that new structure its characteristic qualities."[14] For Freud, this particular attitude of normal masculinity, in and of itself, does represent a developmental advance beyond feminine attachment to archaic objects and illusions. That said, individuals remain at risk for a return of the repressed father, since they are still dependent upon his internalized standards and values.

It must be remembered that, for Freud, anytime there is a return of the repressed father of childhood there is simultaneously a return of the repressed father of the primal horde. What we are talking about, then, is the return of a repressed composite image or psychical representation, made up of characteristics derived from both the primal father and the father of childhood. Freud believed that this repressed image of the father manifests itself, again and again, within both the life of the individual and the collective life of the species. A religious believer, as Ricoeur suggested, who willingly and even gladly accepts the moral condemnation of a stern and punishing Deity, rather than face an existence that is potentially unconsoled and unprotected, would constitute an *individual* manifestation of the repressed oedipal father. In terms of a *collective* manifestation of the repressed oedipal father, Freud could have pointed to Nazi Germany, as a perfect example of what happens when nations of individuals willingly sacrifice their individuality to leaders who demand unwavering loyalty and devotion. This is precisely why normal masculinity, though a progressive step in the right direction, is not enough. Until there is an unmitigated dissolution of the Oedipus Complex within the human psyche, we can expect individuals to at times empty themselves into the heavens, or, more unsettlingly, into totalitarian and megalomaniacal national leaders.

Freud, therefore, was convinced that the dissolution of the Oedipus Complex, in which it is "smashed to pieces," will be a fundamental prelude to a more advanced and enlightened period of human evolution. Not that many of us, female *or* male, experience a successful dissolution of the Oedipus Complex. If this were the case, there would be little, if any need for religious faith, totalitarian leaders, and psychoanalysis. The day of ideal masculinity, when the scientific spirit supersedes the need for religion, is still on the distant horizon, which is why psychoanalysis must continue its work of helping individuals lessen their dependence on psychical images of the repressed oedipal father. "The 'dissolution' of the Oedipus complex," writes Ricoeur, "is attained only with the notion of an order of things stripped of any paternal coefficient, an order that is anonymous and impersonal."[15] Van Herik puts it this way:

> If the superego replaces the father and other authorities to domi-
> nate the son, he has not overcome the father complex but has
> merely internalized it. If, however, the Oedipus complex could be
> destroyed in the id and if the superego which replaces the com-
> plex could become gradually emancipated from its particular
> paternal origins, the Freudian ideal, the primacy of the indepen-
> dent intelligence which submits itself only to impersonal *Ananke*,
> would be possible. The progressive depersonalization of the su-
> perego, which is also its desexualization, is discussed in the con-
> texts of Freud's analyses of anxiety, where he describes the mental
> forces which make men afraid and thereby dominate them.[16]

We might tack on to the end of this quote the following: the mental forces that make human beings afraid and thereby dominate them, *in the person of a tyrannical God or in the person of a totalitarian leader*.

What Van Herik and Ricoeur are both describing is the Freudian goal for the human species, namely, the emancipation of the superego or conscience from its paternal origins—both ontogenetic and phylogenetic—which is preparatory to a more advanced state of reality characterized by an order of things stripped of any paternal coefficient. We might, at this point, want to ask, What about a *maternal* coefficient? For Freud, the question would demonstrate a profound lack of insight and understanding about the nature of the human psyche. Recall Freud's debate with Rolland, concerning the origin of the need for religion. Rolland, as we learned earlier, was of the opinion that the *fons et origio*, the "primary source" of the need for religious faith was somehow connected to the "oceanic feeling," an ineffable longing for a return to the original state of oneness with the mother. Freud strongly disagreed, for two reasons: (1) once the threat of castration enters the developmental picture, the paternal coefficient of protection, from that moment on, will *always* overshadow and be more compelling than the maternal coefficient of consolation; and (2) paternity represents a cultural advance over maternity, the triumph of the rational and enlightened intellect over the primitive senses. This is what Van Herik refers to as Freud's "hierarchy of religio-cultural attitudes." In this hierarchy of attitudes, paternity is more valuable than maternity, since it corresponds to a new reign of intellect.

Maternity, according to Freud, represents a regressive step backward into the world of sense, feeling, and illusion, into the world of psychical attachment to, and dependence on, parental imagoes and representations. Not that the present age of normal masculinity, even with paternity superseding maternity, is the crowning achievement of human evolution. As long as the repressed image of the oedipal father continues to make its return, either in the form of an oppressive God or a totalitarian leader of a nation or peoples, human beings will continue to be dominated by the father complex. This can only mean that the superego is not completely emancipated from its primitive ontogenetic and phylogenetic origins.

If human beings were in possession of a fully emancipated and fully depersonalized superego, then they would be witnessing the dawning of a new age, the age of ideal masculinity, when human beings as a whole experience the total triumph of intellect over illusion. And what, exactly, will get us to the new age of ideal masculinity? According to Freud, it will take progressive detachment from the oedipal father, who, even at present, still manages to dominate the human psyche. The fact that human beings still long for and expect eternal protection from a consoling heavenly Father is, for Freud, all the empirical data that is needed to confirm the view that the oedipal father is still very much alive and well. One can, without too much difficulty, begin identifying certain similarities between Freud's theory of gender and his theory of religion. These similarities will be even more obvious, after we have examined Van Herik's analysis of Freud's work on femininity.

■ FEMININITY AND THE PLEASURE PRINCIPLE ■

Before making connections between gender psychology and religious psychology in Freudian theory, we must first have a very clear understanding of Freud's view of femininity. As we learned earlier, Freud's view of female development is less than flattering. Recall that he likened the psychology and sexuality of women to a dark and mysterious continent. Maybe, on the one hand, this could be a reflection of the times in which Freud was living, as Gay has suggested; he simply never adjusted his old-fashioned views of women to a new and more progressive age. This, however, is a rather generous and charitable interpretation. Rieff, on the other hand, took a less charitable view, suggesting that it is too simplistic to say that Freud was merely echoing the "masculine protest" of his day and age. Instead, Rieff believes, as does Van Herik, that Freud's misogyny was more than cultural prejudice; it had a vital intellectual function in his system, in his psychology of gender and, as we will see, in his psychology of religion. Moreover, it is absolutely essential that we have, along with a firm understanding of Freud's pejorative view of femininity, an understanding of the conclusions he draws from this view. To put this in the form of a question, What is it, exactly, about femininity that makes it such a "dark continent," so difficult to grasp and understand? As we will see, femininity, for Freud, is not so mysterious and incomprehensible after all. On the contrary, he has some rather clear ideas about its fundamental nature, and about its impact upon the evolution of Western culture.

For starters, and most importantly, Freud was convinced that femininity represented, not the renunciation of primary pleasure, but rather its perpetual gratification. Van Herik's word for this perpetual gratification of primary pleasure is *fulfillment.* Thus, we can begin to formulate something of an equation: as masculinity is allied with the renunciation of primary instinct and pleasure, so femininity is allied with its gratification and fulfillment. On the surface, this may not seem like much of a problem—we have, after all, been told that men are from Mars and women are from Venus—until we stop to ask ourselves, What is the nature of this primary pleasure that women seem to unabashedly enjoy in perpetuity? "In Freud's view," writes Van Herik, "femininity in a woman allows her to experience gratification that is re-nounced in ideal masculine development because the feminine attitude re-tains a dependent and consoling libidinal tie to parental figures."[17] As a result, the feminine attitude, because of its retention of libidinal ties to parental figures, must represent, or so it would seem, a regressive step back-ward from the present point of cultural and psychological evolution.

We have managed, as a culture, to establish an order of things stripped of any maternal coefficient—the present androcentric state of normal mas-culinity—and it is really only a matter of time before we institute a new order of things stripped of any and all parental coefficients, maternal *and* paternal—the future state of ideal masculinity. It is little wonder, then, that Freud saw femininity as a dark continent, for it represents, in contrast to normal or ideal masculinity, a very direct link to the world of sense and feeling as well as the perpetuation of libidinal ties to parental figures. And sense, feeling and libidinal attachment to parental figures are, in Freud's view, stum-bling blocks to the "business" and progressive evolution of culture. "Women," observes Van Herik, "are integral to the sensual substratum which must be suppressed in order to get on with the business of the ascendant culture. Once again, pleasure and reality are opposed, and femininity represents and partakes in these psychological modes that masculinity must renounce."[18]

It is important to recognize that when Van Herik uses the terms, *masculinity* and *femininity*, in relation to men and women, she, like Freud, is referring to the *psychical consequences* of the anatomical distinction between the sexes. Masculinity and femininity, then, refer to something more than the anatomical or biological status of individuals, something beyond their status as *male* or *female* members of the human race. Van Herik, to be more specific, uses "the term gender to refer to mental femininity and masculinity in Freud's theories," the connotation being that "masculinity and femininity are psychical attitudes that have cultural roots and consequences."[19] Thus, Van Herik's method is to separate the *biology* of sex differences—male and female—from the *psychology* of gender—masculinity and femininity. Drawing from feminist theory, she reminds us that gender, or the psychology of mas-culinity and femininity, is a culture's interpretation of the meaning of the anatomical or biological differences between the sexes. And, as Ricoeur has made clear, since we as a culture have internalized so much of Freud's theory, it matters a great deal that we acquire a more thorough understanding of his psychology of gender, of the psychological consequences of being male or female.

Van Herik explains that "in asking what Freud's theory of gender differences was, I am asking what Freud found to be the *psychical* difference made by the fact of sex distinction for persons of both sexes, when psychoanalytic method was used to answer the question."[20] The fact that classical psychoanalysis is not as prominent as it was in Freud's day does not mean we can treat it or Freud dismissively. Because we have internalized so many psychoanalytic assumptions—for instance, there are deeper unconscious forces at work within the human psyche; "Freudian slips," whether verbal or nonverbal, are purposeful and therefore meaningful; children, and not only adults, are sexual beings; and so forth—it is, Van Herik argues, absolutely essential that we return again and again to Freud's writings on gender and to his interpretation of the meaning of sex differences.

What we discover, when we delve into Freud's interpretation of the meaning of sex differences, or, in his words, the meaning of the anatomical distinction between the sexes, is that masculinity is more valuable, culturally, than femininity. Masculinity, according to Freud, *renounces* the illusion of libidinal attachment to parental figures, while femininity indulges in the illusion. If, in Western culture, masculinity can somehow manage to completely triumph over femininity, then, in turn, intellect will triumph over sense, reason over feeling and emotion, material reality over psychical reality, independence over dependence, and detachment and separation over attachment. This, of course, begs the very same question Rizzuto posed in chapter 3, Is there such a thing as healthy and mature attachment? Freud would have answered Rizzuto's question with a qualified, "Yes": there is such a thing as mature attachment, as long as the object of one's affection is *external* rather than internal, and exists in the present rather than in the past. What Freud had in mind, in terms of mature attachment, was "object-love," which he associated exclusively with masculinity. This is an anaclitic love, or an active love, directed outward, usually toward a *feminine* object. In contrast, femininity, in the Freudian view, is more representative of a subjective or narcissistic love, a love that is libidinally cathected to *internal* objects, most notably the psychical images of one's parents.

Rizzuto's case study of Fiorella Domenico would seem to illustrate this narcissistic love: by maintaining a libidinal attachment to the image of her father, Fiorella could take pleasure in the illusion of eternal consolation and protection. In other words, Fiorella's was a subjective love, a love of, at bottom, her own physical and emotional safety and security. While she *said* she loved her father, her husband, and her God—that is, while it seemed that she was in possession of an object-love—what she really *meant*, if we examine her case psychodynamically, was that she loved her own comfort and peace of mind. Nor would Freud consider Fiorella's case all that unusual; she is, after all, illustrative of the feminine attitude. Freud, in his essay, "On Narcissism: An Introduction," distinguishes this feminine attitude from the masculine attitude:

> A comparison of the male and female sexes then shows that there are fundamental differences between them in respect of their type of object-choice, although these differences are of course not universal. Complete object-love of the attachment type is, properly speaking, characteristic of the male. It displays the marked sexual overvaluation which is doubtless derived from the child's original narcissism and thus corresponds to a transference of that narcissism to the sexual object. . . . A different course is followed in the type of female most frequently met with, which is probably the purest and truest one. With the onset of puberty the maturing of the female sexual organs, which up till then have been in a condition of latency, seems to bring about an intensification of the original narcissism, and this is unfavourable to the development of a true object-choice with its accompanying sexual overvaluation . . . strictly speaking, it is only themselves that such women love with an intensity comparable to that of the man's love for them. Nor does their need lie in the direction of loving, but of being loved; and the man who fulfills this condition is the one who finds favour with them.[21]

Women, then, by and large, never entirely relinquish or abandon their original narcissism. Although trying to appear open-minded on the subject of femininity—"these differences are of course *not universal*," or "A different course is followed in the *type* of female most frequently met with"—Freud had no doubt whatsoever that women, *universally*, are the bearers of an original narcissism that is unfavorable to the development of a more mature and healthy form of attachment. Freud did concede that there were other types of women, in particular those women who want something more from life than being the passive recipient of a man's object-love. And, in fairness to Freud, he did seem to sympathize with the "unconventional woman," who must somehow try to find a way to stay happy in a patricentric world where male proactivity and female passivity are considered the fundamental norms.[22] However, if this "other type" of woman were to make a move toward greater independence, toward the *masculine* ideal of separation and individuation, she would necessarily be exposing herself to the Freudian charge of "penis envy." Thus, while Freud seemed to sympathize with the woman who does not fit the conventional mold of Western culture, he did not give her any room, theoretically and clinically, to move beyond her unhappy predicament.

Freud, it is fair to say, situated the modern woman in what amounts to a double bind. The message seems to go something like this: it is really unfortunate that most women cannot manage to renounce their original narcissistic love, but if they do attempt to renounce it, by exchanging their narcissistic love for an object-love, they will find themselves standing accused, by Freud *and* Western culture, of being a masculine wanna-be. Or, as Van Herik puts it, women, on the one hand, "were praised for accepting femininity," while, on the other hand, they were told (by Freud and the culture) that "it was an inadequate stance": "If a woman rejected femininity she was neurotic; if she accepted it, she was not successfully human."[23] Therefore, except for the occasional "unconventional woman," women are the universal bearers of an original narcissistic love. Freud, rather puzzlingly, likens the narcissism of femininity to that of a child, an animal, a criminal, and a comedian:

> The importance of this type of woman for the erotic life of mankind is to be rated very high. . . . For it seems very evident that another person's narcissism has a great attraction for those who have renounced part of their own narcissism and are in search of object-love. The charm of a child lies to a great extent in his narcissism, his self-contentment and inaccessibility, just as does the charm of certain animals which seem not to concern themselves about us, such as cats and the large beasts of prey. Indeed, even great criminals and humorists, as they are represented in literature, compel our interest by the narcissistic consistency with which they manage to keep away from their ego anything that would diminish it. It is as if we envied them for maintaining a blissful state of mind—an unassailable libidinal position which we ourselves have since abandoned.[24]

Now what do we make of all this? Since women, in Freudian theory, represent the world of sensuality, primary pleasure, and narcissistic love, they must not be very different from children in terms of their psychical development. Indeed, Freud had little doubt that the psyche of a woman bears a striking resemblance to the psyche of a child. In his work, *Three Essays on the Theory of Sexuality*, Freud wrote that "there are some who have never got over their parents' authority and have withdrawn their affection from them either incompletely or not at all. They are mostly girls, who, to the delight of their parents, have persisted in all their childish love far beyond puberty."[25] That a woman *does not* "smash to pieces" her Oedipus Complex, *does not* begin to dissolve it but rather maintains the libidinal ties to her parents, is, for Freud, an indication that women are, psychically, very much like a *pre*oedipal child.

Van Herik points out that in the case of ideal masculinity, or, to a lesser extent, in the case of normal masculinity, the boy, through a masculine protest against becoming "feminine," dissolves the "parental attachments of his Oedipus complex" and replaces those libidinal attachments with the internalized superego. Not so in the case of the girl. She, according to Freud, establishes her femininity, not by dissolving her Oedipus Complex, but by entering it. "In this situation," writes Van Herik, "the father and later paternal figures are objects to which she is passively attached. The father figure remains external instead of being internalized and depersonalized."[26] This would certainly seem to be an accurate description of Fiorella: her father, her husband, and her God are all paternal figures to which, through the direct continuity of affect and emotion, she is passively attached.

As we saw in chapter 1, the key ingredient missing from the young girl's Oedipus Complex is the threat and the fear of castration. What this means, of course, is that the young girl does not share with the young boy a similar sense of urgency, when it comes to dissolving the primary attachments to parental figures. Fearing castration, the boy has no choice but to abandon primary libidinal attachments to the mother—the wish to possess her—and to the father—the wish to drive him away. True, he internalizes the standards and values of the father, by way of the superego, but this is more of a *secondary* attachment to the father. In fact, it is not so much an attachment to the father as it is an attachment to the standards and values of the father's *culture*. The boy smashes to pieces the desire to possess his mother and to eliminate his father and thereby dissolves all primary libidinal attachments. In so doing, he identifies with the norms of the father, which is another way of saying that he identifies with the values of the culture. And thus a third agency comes into existence within the boy's developing psyche: the superego.

The young girl, however, does not face the same threat of castration. As a result, she does not, according to Freud, feel the same need to sever the primary libidinal ties to parental figures. Instead, the primary ties to parental figures actually become intensified, negatively, toward the mother—feelings of resentment for not being born with a penis—and positively, toward the father—the wish to be the bearer of the father's child. Femininity, then, as Van Herik sees it, "remains ever in the shadow of, and in need of love from, a paternal figure, a situation which, for Freud, makes feminine women lack the independent superego that has cultural value."[27] Freud, in the *New Introductory Lectures on Psycho-analysis*, puts it this way:

> What happens with a girl is . . . the castration complex prepares for the Oedipus complex instead of destroying it; the girl is driven out of her attachment to her mother through the influence of her envy for the penis and she enters the Oedipus situation as though into a haven of refuge. In the absence of fear of castration the chief motive is lacking which leads boys to surmount the Oedipus complex. Girls remain in it for an indeterminate length of time; they demolish it late and, even so, incompletely. In these circumstances the formation of the super-ego must suffer; it cannot attain the strength and independence which give it its cultural significance, and feminists are not pleased when we point out to them the effects of this factor upon the average feminine character.[28]

The implication here is that there is both a *masculine* protest against femininity, or a protest against becoming an emasculated male, and a *feminine* protest against it, for being an emasculated female. Van Herik observes that "in [Freud's] view, boys and girls, men and women, alike carry on, in their mental lives, a 'repudiation of femininity'."[29] If this begins to sound familiar, it should, since Van Herik acknowledges her indebtedness to previous feminist interpretations of Freud and psychoanalysis. She informs us that in attempting "to see how Freud accounts for gender asymmetry analytically and to decide whether this account is useful. . . . I have drawn on [the work of Juliet Mitchell]."[30] Mitchell, in her work, *Psychoanalysis and Feminism*, had argued that in a patriarchal society, *everyone's* unconscious, male or female, repudiates femininity or at least lodges some form of protest against a feminine attitude. Moreover, Mitchell believes that since the unconscious is the manifestation of "mankind's transmission and inheritance of his social (cultural) laws," and since, in a patricentric culture, the image of the oedipal father is at the heart of psychical reality, the logical conclusion is that the repressed oedipal father is "the mental representation of the reality of society."[31]

It is apparent that Mitchell situates herself within the second category of feminists, comprised of those individuals who, while recognizing the inherent sexism within Freudian theory, still believe that Freud can teach us a great deal about the gender asymmetry of Western culture. What Freud can teach us, specifically, is that our views of gender are more than conscious attitudes; they are, in a very fundamental sense, deeply embedded in the Western psyche. These views of masculinity and femininity are, according to Nancy Chodorow, "early developed, unconscious, complex psychic formations, transformed and often built into fundamental character, and are not simply conscious attitudes imposed by a patriarchal society, to be dealt with by reassurance, pointing to the effects of patriarchy, or convincing women to feel better."[32] Mitchell, Chodorow, and Van Herik would all agree that what has been built, first and foremost, into the fundamental character of the Western psyche, is the image of the repressed oedipal father, thanks, at least in part, to the theorizing of Freud.

What we discover is that masculinity and femininity, in a patricentric culture, are defined by their relation to the mental representation of the repressed oedipal father. The young boy, fearing the wrath of his father, for certain illicit thoughts and fantasies, *actively* renounces the primary pleasure he associates with his parents and his libidinal ties to them. The young girl, on the other hand, is not forced out of necessity—that is, out of the fear of castration—to renounce the pleasure principle and to embrace the reality principle to the same appreciable extent. "Therefore, in relation to the father figure, femininity allows fulfillment whereas masculinity requires renunciation."[33]

Again, we can make a case for the importance of the mental representation of the repressed *preoedipal mother*. Object relations theorists, like Rizzuto and D. W. Winnicott, have been trying for quite some time now to give us a more balanced psychoanalytic theory of human development, one that places as much, if not more importance on maternal images and representations. And while object relations theory, and other neo-Freudian schools of thought, have served as important correctives to classical Freudian theory and its emphasis on the primacy of the oedipal father, the fact is that we as a culture have yet to internalize these other schools of thought to the extent that we have internalized classical psychoanalysis. The repressed father complex, articulated by Freud, is still the dominant mental representation of the reality of Western culture. And, in relation to this mental representation, masculinity, as Van Herik has pointed out, *actively* renounces all primary libidinal ties while femininity *passively* allows their fulfillment. She states very succinctly that "femininity and attachment to the father are correlative," while "masculinity precludes attachment to the father."[34] Said another way, "women themselves, who achieve (or fail to achieve) psychical femininity, not only represent, but also *experience*, fulfillments which the successful development of masculinity precludes."[35]

We are now in a position to make certain connections between Freud's psychology of gender and his psychology of religious faith, connections that by now are rather obvious. Before making these connections, in the final portion of this chapter, it is important to recall Freud's guiding critical principle: the renunciation of all primary pleasures and illusions, and the education to reality. Indeed, the fact that Freud has consistently located the psychical qualities of femininity "closer to wish than to reality, to narcissism than to object love, to pleasure than to reality, to fulfillment than to renunciation,"[36] has hardly boded well for women. The fact that he will associate the very same psychical qualities with the religious attitude does not, as we will now see, bode well for religious believers.

■ FEMININITY AND RELIGIOUS FAITH ■

Freud's description of femininity, or the feminine attitude, should give us pause, for it is strikingly similar to his description of the psychical attitude of the religious believer. Those who are psychologically feminine—women— and those who are psychologically religious—believers—share, within the context of Freudian theory, the very same psychical properties: "a weak superego, a poorly developed sense of morality, a restricted intellect, opposition to cultural advance, insufficient respect for reality, *Ananke* and *Logos*."[37] This is especially true of the *Christian* believer, as described by Freud in *The Future of an Illusion*. The *Jewish* believer, on the other hand, represents something of a more sophisticated and advanced psychical position, one which, while not as advanced as the renunciatory scientific spirit, is still a marked improvement over the illusory position of the Christian. What Freud had in mind here is not so much a conventional Jewish faith—whether Orthodox, Conservative, or Reform Judaism—but rather a reconstructed Judaism otherwise known as Mosaic monotheism.

Freud described the features of this Mosaic monotheism in his last major work, aptly titled, *Moses and Monotheism*. "The book," according to

Ricoeur, "contains an impressive number of hazardous hypotheses."[38] This is something of an understatement. Among the more hazardous hypotheses are that (1) Moses was an Egyptian—not only culturally, as we see in the Hebrew Scriptures and Hollywood films, but biologically; (2) that Moses was murdered by the Jews; and (3) that the Yahwistic religion, to a large extent, was the medium for the revival of an "Egyptianized" monotheism. If the latter two hypotheses ring a bell, it might be because what Freud was referring to was the familiar theme of the return of the repressed. And what returns, specifically, is the repressed image of the murdered father of the primal horde as well as the repressed image of the murdered father of the Jewish people, Moses, with both coalescing into the image of Yahweh.

The most hazardous hypothesis of all may very well be Freud's view that Mosaic monotheism grew out of actual historical events. However, Sander L. Gilman has suggested that it could not have been otherwise: Freud needed, for example, the murder of Moses "to be a 'real' event. It had to be as real as the anti-Semitic actions taking place outside his apartment house in the Berggasse . . . as real as the abuse felt on the streets, in the parks, at the university."[39] Freud's point in all of this is that the monotheism of Moses, not to mention modern-day Judaism, represents a progressive step forward, in terms of cultural and intellectual development. How so? Freud put it this way: "The religion which began with the prohibition against making an image of God develops more and more in the course of centuries into a religion of instinctual renunciations."[40] This, of course, reminds us of Yahweh's rather cryptic response to Moses' inquiry about Yahweh's identity: "I am who I am" (see Exod. 3:14). In contrast, Jesus was very forthright about praying to Abba or his "heavenly Father," seemingly encouraging future generations of believers to do the same. Thus, for Freud, the Mosaic prohibition against imaging God, externally or internally, represents at least a partial triumph of intellect over sense perception, of thinking over feeling. The complete and ultimate triumph of intellectuality over sensuality, however, awaits the coming of the age of science.

Human civilization, at least in the West, would have seen the dawning of this new progressive era, if it were not for the fact that there has been a mass and prolonged regression to a more primitive state, as illustrated by the last two millennia of Christian history. Christianity, for Freud, with its emphasis on God the *Father* Almighty, represents the retardation of intellectuality, while Judaism (at least the Judaism of Freud's creation) represents a partial triumph of intellectuality. The renunciatory scientific spirit of a postreligious age will signal the complete and ultimate triumph of the intellect over the senses. In the words of Van Herik, "Belief in Christian ideas is seen as functioning to fulfill wishes for protection and as resulting in restriction of intellect," whereas "the stringent intellectual renunciations that began and were continued within the Jewish tradition have, in Freud's view, strengthened spiritual and intellectual (*geistig*) faculties, thereby ushering in valuable psychological and cultural advances."[41]

Van Herik is quick to point out that Freud was juxtaposing the renunciatory ethic of Judaism with the illusions of the Christian tradition with which he was most familiar, namely, central European Catholicism. Freud, it must be understood, formulated his interpretation of religion on the basis of his direct and personal experience and knowledge of Judaism and Catholicism, apparently without taking into account the psychical effects of Protestantism. "It is likely," Van Herik observes, "that [Freud] selected traditions for study which seemed to him to fit the different evaluations which his psychoanalytic thought had already attached to fulfillments and renunciations, to femininity and masculinity." He showed "no interest, for example, in the psychical results of the Reformation, many of which could be considered renunciatory and critical of 'feminine' components of Catholicism even in Freud's own terms."[42]

Jung, for example, had written a great deal about the absence of the feminine in Protestant theology—for instance, the diminishing influence, if not nonexistence of the theology of Theotokos, or anything having to do with Mary, the "bearer of God." Freud, it appears, was guilty of "prooftexting," of examining only that which confirms what is already believed. He was, after all, looking for two forms of religious expression that simply served to verify and reinforce certain *preexisting* views. Chief among these views was the conviction that renunciation is an advance over fulfillment, intellect an advance over sensuality and emotion, reality an advance over pleasure, and masculinity an advance over femininity. The conclusion we can draw from this is that the religious traditions of Judaism—that is, Mosaic monotheism—and Christianity—that is, central European Catholicism—simply fit the different evaluations that psychoanalysis had *already* attached to previously researched phenomena.

"We are now," according to Van Herik, "in a position . . . to discover that these apparently tangential aspects of [Freud's] argument point to deeper theoretical relationships between fulfillment, femininity, and the psychical position of Christian believers as described in *The Future of an Illusion*, and between renunciation, masculinity, and the psychical position of the inheritors of Mosaic tradition in *Moses and Monotheism*."[43] The psychical position of the Christian believer, as it is described by Freud in *The Future of an Illusion,* is practically identical to the psychical position of femininity. And, the psychical position of the Jewish believer, as it is described by Freud in *Moses and Monotheism,* is practically identical to the psychical position of normal masculinity. In case there is any doubt that Freud was linking the psychical attitude of renunciatory masculinity with the tradition of Mosaic monotheism, it might do us well to keep in mind the original titles Freud gave to his final work, before eventually deciding on *Moses and Monotheism,* as a final title for the book: *Der Mann Moses, ein historischer Roman,* or The man Moses, a historical novel, and *Der Mann Moses und die monotheistische Religion: drei Abhandlungen,* or The man Moses and the monotheistic religion: three essays.

Freud himself has taught us that everything we say or do is purposeful, that it is full of meaning on many different levels. So, the fact that he had actually considered including *Der Mann* in the title seems indicative of what was going through his mind at the time. By 1939, the year *Moses and Monotheism* was published, Freud was living in a very different world, and was keenly aware that, in his words, "the feminists" had made inroads into various fields of research, including the field of psychoanalysis. Thus, Freud felt compelled to drop *Der Mann* from the title, in deference to the opinion of "the feminists." Nevertheless, the *spirit* of the book remains the same: The monotheism associated with Moses, with its renunciation of illusions, represents a cultural and intellectual advance over wish-fulfilling Christianity, which is exactly what gives masculinity its advantage over femininity.

Not that this particular form of monotheism, or contemporary Judaism for that matter, happens to be the telos of Western culture, the end to which we strive. This cannot be the case, for the Mosaic monotheism of Freudian theory and the Judaism of the present day and age are representative of the psychical position of *normal* masculinity. For us to get to the next, more advanced stage of human evolution, we will necessarily have to renounce *all* attachment to a divine being, whether imaged or not. This will be none other than the age of reason, when the position of ideal masculinity eclipses the position of normal masculinity, when science eclipses, once and for all, religious faith. "The psychical structure of Moses' heirs," writes Van Herik, "is like that of [normal] masculinity which is still under the sway of the father complex but which has differentiated itself from prior, wishful phases through renunciations." This, for Freud, is an advance over previous psychical positions, such as femininity, but it still does not go far enough. "The form of deconverted conviction" that Freud was looking for, "that corresponds to the psychical structure of 'ideal masculinity'," resembles "the postreligious scientist and scholar who is described in *The Future of an Illusion*."[44]

As we know by now, women, in Freudian theory, are still very much under the sway of the pleasure principle. Without the threat of castration, they have less reason to renounce the primary attachments to parental figures. But even with the threat of castration, there is, in the case of normal masculinity, an unwillingness to completely let go of the pleasure principle. There are still plenty of *male* religious believers, which, in Freud's view, is a sure sign that the pleasure principle, albeit in a modified form, lives on even within the context of normal masculinity. Van Herik notes that "those under the sway of religious ideas have failed to dissolve the Oedipus complex in the ideal masculine way; for them, the pleasure principle rules, and they construct reality on the basis of libidinal ties to fathers."[45] This is expressly true of the *Christian* believer, and, to a lesser yet noticeable extent, of the *Jewish* believer.

Through the resourcefulness of Van Herik's research, "we have seen that, for Freud, intellectual primacy is not only the psychological but also the masculine and cultural ideal. It is an ideal that, for similar reasons, the believer and those who are psychologically feminine cannot achieve."[46] In Freudian theory, women and religious believers are both psychologically feminine, for both groups adopt a passive and submissive position toward father figures. Peter Gay's observation, that Freud was merely a gentleman who never could or would catch on to the spirit of the new age and the more progressive views on femininity, fails to capture the essence of Freudian thought. Even Rieff's observation, that Freud's pejorative view of women is more than the masculine protest of his day and age, is more personal misogyny than cultural prejudice, does not delve deep enough into the presuppositional world of psychoanalysis. What is at the heart of psychoanalytic theory, according to Van Herik, is not so much misogyny and the masculine protest—although both are certainly present, in one form or another—but the critical principle of renunciation, the renunciation of all wish-fulfilling illusions and all primary libidinal attachments.

For Freud, the critical principle is most apropos to the study of femininity and to the study of religious faith, since, in his mind, the two psychical attitudes are virtually the same. As Van Herik puts it, "once the dynamics of renunciation and fulfillment are inseparable from gender—and gender is their instigation and their result—Freud's diagnoses of mental relationships to gods are not separable from gender either. In Freud's texts, gender psychology and religious psychology are inseparable."[47] Whether we are studying Freud's work on gender or his interpretation of religious faith, the fact is we can detect, in either context, a hierarchy of religio-cultural attitudes. For example, "paralleling Freud's belief that science is superior to religion is another assumption: the superiority of masculinity over femininity." David M. Wulff continues:

> Judith Van Herik astutely points out that, together, these presup-positions establish a "hierarchy of religio-cultural attitudes," or-dered according to the degree of instinctual renunciation. At the bottom of Freud's hierarchy are the naive Christian worshipers who, in a submissive, feminine attitude, seek fulfillment through personal relation with a loving powerful Father-God. At the second level are the Jewish worshipers who in a more active, masculine manner obey the father's demands for renunciation of instinctual wishes, thereby instigating various intellectual, cul-tural and ethical advances. Beyond this attitude of "normal masculinity"—which, still dominated by a repressed Oedipus complex, borders on the neurotic—lies the highest level, of "ideal masculinity." Here, the Oedipus complex has been dissolved and reality becomes depersonalized; renunciation has finally allowed the emergence of the postreligious, scientific outlook. Thus we see more clearly how fundamentally Freud's negative view of femininity, as well as his treatment of masculinity as the univer-sal norm and ideal, has guided his interpretations of religion.[48]

The religious attitude, therefore, which is grounded in the fundamental belief in a kind and loving Providence, is, for Freud, psychically like the feminine attitude toward fathers and paternal figures. And this holds true, whether the feminine attitude is manifested in the psychical position of the *pre*oedipal boy or that of the *post*oedipal girl. As Van Herik, Mitchell, and Chodorow have all demonstrated, when the dominant social reality is that of patriarchy, "everyone, consciously or unconsciously, repudiates his or her own mental femininity," for "femininity is the passive love relationship to father figures, which infantile masculinity must renounce as a precondition for real-izing itself as socialized masculinity."[49] Since he is guided by the critical prin-ciple of renunciation of any and all illusions, Freud can only see religious faith and the feminine attitude as two peas of the very same psychical pod.

What we learn from Van Herik's work is that one cannot fully under-stand Freud's interpretation of religious faith as psychological projection without having a thoroughgoing knowledge of his psychology of gender. To be sure, "the feminine relationship to the father is like that of the naive believer in the Christian father-god as it is portrayed in *The Future of an Illusion*. . . . Both are charged with restricting intellectual, moral, and cultural development, and for similar reasons: longing for the father is appeased rather than renounced."[50] Van Herik, as Wulff suggested, has indeed gotten to the bottom of the Freudian presuppositional world, by identifying a hierarchy of religio-cultural attitudes ordered according to the degree of instinctual renunciation. As noted earlier, Van Herik's impressive research would have been further strengthened if she had disclosed where she, personally, stands on the issue of Freud and feminism. For example, does she see him and his theory as prototypically sexist, or does she believe his theory can be used for feminist construction? One can certainly infer that Van Herik, too, would give Freud a partial "yes," especially his description of gender psychology and religious psychology, as they are formed in the context of a patricentric culture. Van Herik, in her own words, puts it this way: Since "[Freud's] psychologies of religion and gender differentiation both rest on paternal etiology," they are accurate "theories of mental religiosity and sexuality within a patricentric and patriarchal mental world."[51]

■ F I V E ■

Beyond Either-or: Toward A Constructive Reengagement with Freud

There should be no question of what Christian theology has to do in this situation. It should decide for truth against safety, even if the safety is consecrated and supported by the churches.

Paul Tillich, *The Courage to Be*

In this book, I have attempted to continue the necessary exploration of the full meaning of recent developments within psychoanalysis, and, more specifically, the full meaning of inquiries into the field of psychoanalysis by scholars of religion. I purposely brought together the work of three theorists—Paul Ricoeur, Ana-Maria Rizzuto, and Judith Van Herik—who have demonstrated, in very different ways, that Freudian theory has been and still is extraordinarily influential in the West, and that it still has significant power vis-à-vis religious faith. Freud, of course, reductively viewed religion as a purely psychological phenomenon, the projection of our own subjectivity onto a perceived cosmic figure with the capacity to fulfill our wish to be eternally protected and consoled. It is little wonder, then, that religious believers have had and still have a difficult time engaging him and his theory of religion as psychological projection. But, as we have seen, others, such as Ricoeur, Rizzuto, and Van Herik, consider it a serious mistake to dismiss Freud outright, simply because he came to an erroneous conclusion about religion, God, and ultimate reality. These three theorists have demonstrated, in very different ways, that the inherent limitations of psychoanalysis do not preclude a serious discussion of its hermeneutical utility.

Building on the work of Ricoeur, Rizzuto, and Van Herik, I have attempted to demonstrate that religious believers can use the Freudian interpretation of religion to establish a way to creatively and imaginatively live within the dialectical tension that develops whenever our belief system is challenged and/or disrupted. What emerges from this study, therefore, is a

constructive approach to the emotional and spiritual tension we experience
as a result of engaging a Freudian, as well as any other hermeneutics of
suspicion. My research, in other words, on Freud's theory of religion as projection, has gone beyond description, explanation, and critique, in an attempt to determine the extent to which Freud's theory can expand, enrich,
and enliven our knowledge of religious faith. Thus, while giving psychoanalysis plenty of opportunity to speak for itself, I have also intentionally
inverted it so that religious believers can use it more to *their* advantage.

Ricoeur, Rizzuto, and Van Herik, as we discovered in chapters 2–4,
argue, in methodologically diverse ways, that believers cannot ignore Freud's
work on religion, even if he does come to an erroneous conclusion about
ultimate reality. Whether or not believers agree with Freud's conclusion about
God and religion, they are, according to each of these scholars, obligated to
converse with him about his theory of the origin of religious faith. None of
these theorists, interestingly enough, becomes, in the process of engaging
Freud and his theory, a full-fledged "convert" to classical psychoanalysis.
However, they could not, following a systematic engagement with psychoanalytic theory, look at religious faith quite the same way again. Believers
should not construe this as something *negative*, for what the engagement
with Freudian theory did was clarify, deepen, and expand the theorists' understanding of the nature of religion.

What this would mean for believers is that an intentional and extended engagement with Freud and his theory could in fact illuminate certain aspects of their religious faith. Rather than assuming that we are being
disloyal to God and to our respective faith traditions, by devoting time and
energy to Freud's interpretation of religion, it might do us well, especially in
light of the work of these particular theorists, to at least entertain the possibility that we may come away from the engagement with a deeper and
greater appreciation of God and of our particular faith tradition. Put more
simply, believers have a unique opportunity to deepen their understanding of
the nature, power, and efficacy of religious faith.

■ METHODOLOGICAL STRATEGIES ■

In chapter 2, Ricoeur noted that Freud's suggestion that psychoanalysis was
responsible for one of the three blows to humankind's universal narcissism
merits serious consideration. For, along with Copernicus, who dealt us a
cosmological humiliation, and Charles Darwin, who dealt us a biological

humiliation, Freud was successful at dealing us a psychological humiliation, demonstrating, through psychoanalysis, that we are not even the ruler of our own psychical world. Any attestation of selfhood, therefore, after Freud, will need to be inseparable from an exercise of suspicion. Moreover, human consciousness becomes a task, a dynamic *Bewusstwerden* or "becoming-consciousness," rather than a *Bewusstsein* or "being-consciousness." All of which has very important implications for religious faith. We could, quite frankly, substitute "religious faith" for "consciousness," and say the same thing: after Freud's critique of religion, religious faith must henceforth become a task, if it is to have credibility in a postmodern world.

What Freud's hermeneutics of suspicion teaches us, if we are willing to pay very close attention, is that religious faith, in any *human* shape or form, will always be the bearer of residual traces of primitive immaturity. This primitive immaturity, according to Ricoeur, is manifested in the believer's wish to be consoled and protected by a God who resembles the psychical image of an early caregiver(s). For example, the exalted Deity, if imaged juxtapositionally with the psychical representation of the oedipal father, will more than likely be a consoling and protective Presence, but, at the same time, will also be an accusatory and punishing Presence. The two—consolation *and* constraint—as Freud pointed out, go hand in hand, anytime one's image of God is psychically modeled after the representation of the father of the oedipal years. This is an unreflective religious faith of the first naïveté, and it is this form of faith in particular that Ricoeur believes stands most in need of Freud's interrogative schooling. The individual, after his or her unexamined faith has been deconstructed, can then begin to reimage a God who does not necessarily rule over nature as an empire, who does not annul death, and who does not redress the afflictions of this life, but who instead surrenders us to the totality of human existence and to the inherent ambiguities of human living.

This, as we learned from Ricoeur, is the capacity of a Freudian hermeneutics of suspicion to refine and purify. Obviously, the implication is that the deconstruction of a religious faith of the first naïveté, at the hands of Freudian theory, is both a loss *and* an opportunity. On the one hand, a Freudian hermeneutics of suspicion has the capacity to challenge and disrupt the believer's religious faith, but, on the other hand, it also has the capacity to enrich, enliven, and ultimately strengthen it. For example, the believer who approaches psychoanalysis with a certain amount of openness and objectivity can learn that a moralistic and punishing God, who protects and consoles but also accuses and punishes, *is* almost certainly a projection of the oedipal father of childhood in response to reactivated feelings of vulnerability and helplessness. Thus, whether or not Freud's theory finds widespread empirical confirmation is really beside the point. When read hermeneutically, the Freudian interpretation of religion does confirm that human beings do at times prefer the moral condemnation of a punishing Deity to an existence that is unprotected and unconsoled. Here is where the believer must be willing to give Freud an unqualified "yes."

Freud, though, as Ricoeur has pointed out, must also be given an unqualified "no," particularly when it comes to the view that ultimate reality is never more than Ananke, or "harsh necessity." Human beings, in the face of such a cold and stark reality, are, according to Freud, morally obligated to resign themselves to the fact that this is the way it is, and stop trying to pretend it could be otherwise. But it can be otherwise, through the grace of human creativity and imagination. Religious believers, whose faith has been enlivened by a Freudian hermeneutics of suspicion, can, at this point, move beyond the Freudian stance of fatalistic resignation in the face of a harsh and cold Ananke, to a more creative, imaginative, and grace-filled way of living on the earth. The believer, then, after giving Freud an informed "yes," can then give him an informed "no," by exchanging a hermeneutics of suspicion for a hermeneutics of purified and strengthened belief and meaning.

In chapter 3, we learned from Rizzuto's clinical method that there really is no monolithic Freudian theory. Rather, there are "two Freuds": the one of science, intellect, and reality, and the one of object relations, the Oedipus Complex, and family relations. Rizzuto, as we saw, deftly resisted the former—the Freud who had said, "No our science is no illusion. But an illusion it would be to suppose that what science cannot give us we can get elsewhere"—while, at the same time, learning from and being guided by the latter—the Freud who reminds us that we can never distance ourselves entirely from the feelings and images of childhood. Rizzuto's approach to Freud was nothing less than a both-and approach. Freudian theory, when it came to the case of Fiorella Domenico, had tremendous explanatory and hermeneutical power. Rizzuto, after working extensively with Fiorella, did uncover a direct and most tenacious continuity of affect or emotion, which was rooted in Fiorella's psychical representation of her father and later extended to images of God and husband. In the language of Ricoeur, here again is where Freud is entitled to an unqualified "yes."

The case of Douglas O'Duffy, on the other hand, is where Freud must be given an unqualified "no." Freud's theory that religious sentiments and feelings always and exclusively surface during the oedipal years had less explanatory power, when it came to Douglas's case. In fact, Romain Rolland's view, that the *fons et orgio*, "the primary source" of religious sentiments lies in the oceanic feeling, the longing for that original preoedipal state of oneness with the universe in the form of the mother, would appear to be a more fitting description of Douglas's situation. Douglas, as Rizzuto discovered during the course of the treatment, was more intent on having a corrective emotional experience of mirroring with his mother (what he also wanted and needed from his God) than on finding consolation and protection from a God who resembled the father of the oedipal years. Those who work in the fields of pastoral care and counseling, spiritual direction, parish or specialized ministry as well as theological or religious education, can be guided by Rizzuto's creative both-and approach to Freudian theory, in order to better understand the developmental history of clients, patients, parishioners, and students.

Rizzuto demonstrated, by applying psychoanalysis to her clinical work with patients, that people's ideas and images of God are at least a partial exaltation of parental imagoes. What this means is that if we decide to dismiss Freud's theory of religion outright, either because we believe it diminishes the transcendent role of God or it diminishes the exalted role of human beings in the created order, then we end up putting ourselves at a disadvantage in our work with those in our care. Our ignorance of God's immanent and intimate psychical role, within the lives of those with whom we are working, means that we are necessarily missing important and valuable pieces of information about the developmental history of these individuals.

Rizzuto, as we saw in chapter 3, took Freud to task for his unyielding and dogmatic view that religion is always neurotic or immature or both. Freud is right, *if* we are talking about an unreflective and unexamined religious faith of the first naïveté. However, if one is in possession of a postcritical faith of the second naïveté, characterized by a transformed and life-giving image of God, then psychoanalysis begins to lose its hermeneutical power. Rizzuto, in other words, disagreed with Freud's view that religious faith is always irrational, but she did find him particularly helpful when it comes to the matter of the psychical juxtaposition of parental representations and images of God. If we, like Rizzuto, can at least initially limit our focus to Freud's work with psychical experience, instead of immediately citing his conclusion about ultimate reality, then we find that he really does have something to teach us about the origins of the human individual's God-image.

Then, in chapter 4, we examined Van Herik's work with Freudian theory, and learned that there are in fact profound similarities between Freud's psychology of women and his psychology of religious believers. Freud's unifying

critical principle, which he applies equally and forcefully to the study of
gender and to the study of religious faith, is *renunciation*; specifically, the
renunciation of all wish-fulfilling illusions and all primary libidinal attachments. This, so it would seem, is exactly what women and Christian believers do *not* do: renounce, respectively, primary libidinal ties to parents and the
wish-fulfilling illusion of a benevolent divine Being. The critical principle of
renunciation, then, is simultaneously applicable to the study of femininity
and to the study of religious faith, since, for Freud, the two psychical attitudes are virtually one and the same. Both attitudes are given to fulfillment,
to gratifying the pleasure principle, rather than to its renunciation and to
growing up into reality. Moreover, once the standards of renunciation and
fulfillment become inseparable from gender, then the analysis of psychical
attachments to God and religious faith is no longer separable from gender.
Van Herik has cogently demonstrated that within the Freudian corpus of
writings gender psychology and religious psychology are inseparable, if not
identical. The religious attitude, for Freud, which is grounded in the steadfast
and fundamental belief in a kind and benevolent Providence, is psychically
indistinguishable from the passive feminine attitude toward fathers and parental figures. Since he is guided by the critical principle of the renunciation
of all wish-fulfilling illusions, Freud can only see religious faith and the
feminine attitude in a rather pejorative light.

Van Herik has astutely called our attention to the inextricable link
between gender psychology and religious psychology, in Freudian theory.
Indeed, Freud's psychology of religion and his psychology of gender both rest
on, in Van Herik's words, "paternal etiology," and are in fact accurate theories of mental religiosity and mental sexuality in the context of a patricentric
mental world. In this context, the woman's relationship to her parents, particularly her father, is like that of the naive believer to a heavenly Parent or
heavenly Father. Freud charges both attitudes with restricting, rather than
advancing intellectual, moral, and cultural development. One cannot, after
reading Van Herik, look at Freud the same way again. Whether we are
examining Freud's theory of religion, his theory of human development or
his psychology of gender, the fact is we will be able to identify, in any of
these contexts, a hierarchy of religio-cultural attitudes ordered according to
the degree of instinctual renunciation. Van Herik, then, engages Freud for
reasons other than trying to determine, like Ricoeur, the hermeneutical utility of Freudian theory, or, like Rizzuto, its clinical utility. More specifically,
instead of trying to determine what Freud can teach us about the psychical
role of God or about our willingness to tolerate moral condemnation in

cause

etiology = αιΤια + λογος

exchange for the promise of eternal security, Van Herik elucidates the intimate connection between Freud's theory of religion as psychological projection and his theory of gender differences.

Though her method is more intellectually neutral than Ricoeur's or Rizzuto's, Van Herik's unique contribution is the unearthing of the Freudian presuppositional world, and the identification of Freud's guiding critical principle: renunciation of all illusions, wish-fulfillments, and primary libidinal attachments. After carefully examining Van Herik's work, we must conclude that religious faith and femininity, in Freudian theory, are indeed linked together through related inner meanings—for instance, primary pleasure, irrationality, projection, and psychical underdevelopment. Believers, then, who long for a consoling Deity to come to them with tender loving care, are not, in Freud's mind, very different from women who seem less willing or able to renounce primary libidinal ties to external and internal parental objects. Despite Freud's devaluation of female development, and despite his pejorative theorizing on the nature of religious faith, Van Herik still challenges us, and rightly so, to return again and again to his writings on religion and gender, in order to discover important clues about present-day attitudes in the West. Said another way, the more we know of Freud and his theory, the more we will know about ourselves as individuals and as a culture.

Religious believers now have in their possession three very different and very distinct methodological strategies for engaging Freud and his theory of religion as psychological projection. For those who work in the field of theological or religious education, for example, Ricoeur's work with Freud can be an invaluable resource, serving as a model for how to apply a Freudian hermeneutics of suspicion to the "text" of the student's religious faith, in hopes of helping the student see the value of exchanging an unreflective faith of the first naïveté for that of a postcritical faith of the second naïveté. This, of course, implies a pedagogical approach of "both-and," in the sense that a hermeneutics of belief and meaning is firmly held in dialectical tension with a hermeneutics of suspicion.

Rizzuto, as noted, resisted delving into the issue of the existence of God or into God's transcendent role. Still, those who practice pastoral counseling, spiritual direction, and spiritually attentive psychotherapy, as well as those who work in the field of parish or specialized ministry, now have a model of how to use Freudian theory in order to better understand the developmental and spiritual history of clients and parishioners. And, for those who feel uncomfortable with the methodological strategies of Ricoeur and Rizzuto, who feel these two theorists have conceded too much to Freud, there is Van Herik's methodologically neutral approach to psychoanalysis. Van Herik, in linking Freudian attitudes toward religious faith and femininity and cultural attitudes toward religious believers and women, demonstrates that in many ways we can come to a better understanding of Western culture and the Western psyche by becoming more familiar with Freud.

Certainly, one methodological size will not fit all, which is why I have included, in this study, three very different theorists who make use of Freud's interpretation of religion in three different and distinct ways. Ricoeur and Rizzuto, then, have supplied us with methodologies—hermeneutical and clinical, respectively—which can best be described as normative and valuational frameworks, from which to engage Freud and his theory of religion. These theorists wanted, not only to *understand* Freud's unique and extraordinary influence in the West, but also to *evaluate* his influence, in terms of the correctness or incorrectness of his theory. In contrast, Van Herik's methodology was more circumscribed, limited to *understanding* the impact of Freud on Western religio-cultural attitudes. While it would be useful for Van Herik, at some point, to take her research an additional step further, into the realm of *evaluation*, she has, for now, given religious believers an important methodological strategy for engaging Freudian theory and, in the process, learning more about themselves and their culture.

The major difference, then, between the first two approaches to Freud—Ricoeur's and Rizzuto's—and the third approach—Van Herik's—is that the former two look at the critical weight of Freudian views in Western culture *and* the correctness or incorrectness of the views themselves, while the latter approach limits itself to cultural analysis, thus stopping short of taking a normative stance toward Freud. When Rizzuto intimates that she follows the "other Freud," the Freud of object relations, the Oedipus Complex, and family relations, and, likewise, when Ricoeur argues that the Freudian hermeneutics of suspicion deserves, in part, an unqualified "yes" from the religious believer, they are taking a normative position toward, not only the cultural weight of Freudian views, but toward the Freudian views themselves.

What Ricoeur and Rizzuto both discover along the way is that, yes, Freud's view of religion has been extraordinarily influential in Western culture, *and*, that yes, Freud's interpretation of religion as psychological projection is at least partially correct. Ricoeur and Rizzuto, as it were, are representative of a more inclusive approach to Freud, one which, in the long run, sets them apart from Van Herik. All three of the theorists, on the one hand, agree that we must understand and come to terms with the degree to which we analyze ourselves through Freud, yet, on the other hand, it is

Ricoeur and Rizzuto who go beyond merely understanding Freud's influence on Western culture and on our religio-cultural attitudes, to evaluating it in terms of its correctness and incorrectness.

Van Herik, to be fair, also seems to want to nudge her readers beyond an either-or framework, beyond either an uncritical and overvalued appreciation of psychoanalysis, or, like certain feminists and religious believers, beyond an attitude of antipathy toward anything having to do with Freud. Van Herik, like Ricoeur and Rizzuto, believes it is important for us to find a more optimal both-and solution: while some of Freud's conclusions about femininity and religious faith are erroneous or offensive or both, we can still acknowledge and come to terms with his influence on Western culture. Ricoeur and Rizzuto, however, go even further, suggesting that while acknowledging the influence of Freud is indeed a first step, more is required.

Specifically, we must *evaluate* his influence, and, in so doing, come to see that while the Freud of object relations, the Oedipus Complex, family relations, and the hermeneutics of suspicion did not get everything right about the psychological and spiritual dynamics of religious faith, he did manage to get some things right. Moreover, when the subject is Freud, whose influential theories of religion and gender have often been regarded as oppressive and offensive, we are obligated to arrive at some sort of conclusion about the correctness or incorrectness of his theory. Freud's theories of religion and gender, in other words, must be understood *and* eventually evaluated, for they will not let us remain neutral.

So why, we may ask, include the work of Van Herik? Would we have been further ahead to limit the critical-analysis portion of this book to the first two theorists—Ricoeur and Rizzuto—who both believe a study of Freud is never complete without an evaluation of the correctness or incorrectness of his theory, and an evaluation of its theoretical, clinical, and hermeneutical utility? I do not think so. Van Herik's analysis of Freud represents something of a middle-ground approach, and may be less threatening to the religious believer who finds it difficult, if not impossible to admit that there is a certain amount of correctness to Freud's interpretation of religion. Certainly, it would be naive to assume that every believer will eventually evolve, by way of Ricoeur, Rizzuto, or some other theorist, to the point where he or she will have little difficulty holding Freudian theory and religious faith in perfect dialectical tension. Some believers, after reading what Ricoeur and Rizzuto have to say about Freud, will likely throw up their hands and say to themselves, "Forget it! I can't be open-minded about Freud and loyal to my religious faith at the same time."

To these religious believers, who either will not or cannot engage the partial correctness of Freud's interpretation of religion, who will only or can only see its glaring and overt incorrectness, Van Herik and her methodology can function as something of an alternative resource, helping believers to at least see that Freud's critique of religion has been and still is influential in the West. While it would certainly be ideal for every religious believer to see the inherent and simultaneous correctness and incorrectness of Freudian theory, the fact is, there will always be believers who find it especially difficult to admit that Freud has anything important and relevant to say about the nature of religious faith. Thus, if total engagement with Freud, the modus operandi of choice for both Ricoeur and Rizzuto, feels overwhelming to religious believers, they may look instead to Van Herik, to at least develop some measure of understanding of Freud's influence on Western culture.

Returning to the context of seminary education, for example, we can attempt to construct a method for how to present Freud and his theories of religion and gender to seminarians. Not every seminarian, it is safe to say, will want to immediately delve into Ricoeur's or Rizzuto's analysis of Freudian theory. Some, no doubt, will find it more than a little unsettling to hear from Ricoeur that a hermeneutics of belief must be firmly held in dialectical tension with a Freudian hermeneutics of suspicion, or, from Rizzuto, that the Freud of science, intellect, and reality must be firmly held in tension with the "other Freud," the Freud of object relations, the Oedipus Complex, and family relations. It might be useful, then, in the context of a presentation or semester course on Freud, to think in terms of introducing the three theorists in reverse: begin with Van Herik's religio-cultural approach to Freud, then move to Rizzuto's clinical approach, and conclude with Ricoeur's hermeneutical approach.

This methodological and pedagogical strategy—Van Herik to Rizzuto to Ricoeur—would give those we are working with time to get used to the idea of Freud being an important influence on Western culture, before having to hold his theory in dialectical tension with religious faith. If we begin with the work of Van Herik, then believers will find themselves initially engaging more objective facts and findings, without having to immediately expose their religious faith to the full impact of a Freudian critique and interpretation. Then, after familiarizing themselves with Van Herik's work, believers may be more able and willing to familiarize themselves with Rizzuto's work with Freud, and her finding that God is always juxtaposed, psychically, with the imagoes and representations of childhood. Finally, after engaging Van Herik and Rizzuto, believers would be prepared to engage Ricoeur and his argument that they are obligated to purify their religious faith of its primitive naïveté, by way of a hermeneutics of suspicion. In the end, this methodological strategy would help believers ease their way into seeing that holding opposing views in dialectical tension leads to greater emotional and spiritual growth and development.

■ SOMETHING RESEMBLING PSYCHICAL SPLITTING? ■

By exploring the work of three theorists who have intentionally engaged psychoanalytic theory, we have seen that it is possible, if not advantageous for believers to hold their religious faith in dialectical tension with Freud's theory of religion. Whether believers apply Ricoeur's hermeneutical method or Rizzuto's clinical method or Van Herik's religio-cultural method to the study of Freud and religion, they will learn much about religion as a cultural phenomenon and about the origins of their own personal religious faith. This study, then, has demonstrated that Freud's theory of religion as psychological projection, if applied astutely to the "text" of religious faith, can be used by the believer to establish a way to creatively live *within* the dialectical tension that develops whenever our belief system is challenged or disrupted, by Freud or by anyone else applying a hermeneutics of suspicion. In engaging Freud's theory of religion, believers, paradoxically, will discover that they have much to gain from the encounter. Freud, it is true, will deconstruct, with little difficulty, an unexamined and unreflective faith of the first naïveté, but this is simply a *means* to the *end* of reconstructing a richer and livelier postcritical faith of the second naïveté.

But what about believers who, even after familiarizing themselves with the methodological strategies of Ricoeur, Rizzuto, and Van Herik, steadfastly refuse to take an objective and open-minded look at Freud's writings on religion? What then? On the surface, at least, believers are simply being loyal to their God or to their religious tradition. Scripture, after all, is very clear about the inherent difficulties of serving more than one master. Believers, accordingly, might feel compelled to choose between *either* the totality of religion *or* the totality of psychoanalysis. This either-or approach, however, seems akin to the phenomenon of psychical compartmentalization, and to the dividing of objects and images into good and bad categories.

Otto Kernberg, the psychoanalyst, refers to this phenomenon as psychical "splitting." Splitting, he suggests, is a very basic and fundamental defensive maneuver, which underlies and fuels all other defensive operations.

The classic manifestation of splitting is the division of external or internal objects into two radically separate groups: an all-good group and an all-bad group. Kernberg points out that the common feature of psychical splitting is "the incapacity to synthesize the positive and negative introjections and identifications," or "the lack of synthesis of contradictory self and object images." He goes on to say that

> Splitting is maintained as an essential mechanism preventing diffusion of anxiety within the ego and protecting the positive introjections and identifications. The need to preserve the good self, and good object images, and good external objects in the presence of dangerous "all bad" self and object images leads to a number of subsidiary defensive operations.[1]

What can occur, then, when the psyche is beset by conflict between diametrically opposed thoughts or images, is that the individual, rather than trying to hold the opposing forces together in dialectical tension, keeps them far apart and therefore experiences a temporary reduction of psychical tension. The use of the word *temporary*, is not accidental, because the individual, from this point on, must be on his or her guard since the negative image has not, as had been hoped, entirely vanished. Instead, the bad or negative images—what Kernberg, using psychoanalytic language, calls "negative introjections and identifications"—have merely gone underground, into the realm of unconsciousness. And, if Freud has taught the Western world anything, it is that just because something is removed from consciousness does not mean that it has gone away. To put this colloquially, the negative psychical image may be out-of-sight, but this is hardly an indication that it is out of mind. The negative or disturbing image, because it is no longer conscious, begins to take on a life of its own.

Since individuals have only arrived at a *temporary* solution, or at a temporary reduction of the psychical tension, they will need to be, from now on, hypervigilant. The bad thoughts or images, which have been repressed, will, from time to time, come to the fore and demand expression. In Freudian terms, there is always the threat of a return of the repressed. The splitting mechanism, then, needs reinforcement, so it falls back upon subsidiary defensive maneuvers—anger, distancing, indifference, denial, projection, rationalization, and so on. Had individuals been committed to holding diametrically opposed images—that is, good and bad ones—together in dialectical tension, or in integrating them into a coherent whole, the ego would have been strengthened. Instead, because the individual resorted to separating the bad from the good, to keeping the two worlds completely apart, the ego has been weakened. Splitting, accordingly, "is a fundamental cause of ego weakness, and as splitting also requires less countercathexis than repression, a weak ego falls back easily on splitting, and a vicious circle is created by which ego weakness and splitting reinforce each other."[2]

I believe that it is not too far-fetched, or even far-fetched at all, to say that something similar happens within the psyche of the religious believer who, ostensibly out of loyalty to God or to a particular faith tradition, refuses to engage Freud even before encountering his writings and theory. Some believers, undoubtedly, will have sufficient ego strength to firmly hold the truth of psychoanalysis in dialectical tension with the truth of religious faith. For other believers, however, the thought of holding the theory of an atheist in tension with their religious faith will be too unsettling, especially if that faith is largely unexamined. The only recourse, then, for the believer unwilling to part with a faith of the first naïveté, will be that of splitting—an all-bad Freudian theory must be kept far apart from an all-good religious faith. Put another way, the believer who is unable or unwilling to hold opposite views in tension, will inevitably resort to the basic and primitive defense of psychical splitting, in order to keep the negative thought or image at bay. And, as we have seen, a vicious circle is created by which ego weakness and splitting reinforce each other.

The religious believer, at this point, might be tempted to say, "It sounds like I'm being judged or pathologized, just because I won't read Freud!" This is certainly not my intention. The lack of psychical integration on the part of the individual with, say, characterological or personality disturbances, and the lack of psychical integration on the part of the religious believer, who refuses to integrate any Freudian theory into his or her belief system, is obviously apples and oranges. Nevertheless, something resembling or akin to psychical splitting is at work within the psyche of the believer who refuses to discuss Freud and religion in the same breath.

Freud, as we all know by now, issued a devastating critique of religion. Thus, it should not come as too much of a surprise if certain believers feel compelled to keep him at arm's length. This emotional distancing, though, could prove costly in the long run, especially if the price is the repetitive weakening of ego and spirit. Indeed, the believer who refuses to part with an unexamined faith of the first naïveté can do nothing but fall back upon the defense of psychical splitting, of keeping an all-bad Freud far removed from an all-good religious faith. Furthermore, it is impossible for this particular believer to understand that a challenge to our religious faith represents, not only a threat, but also a valuable opportunity. When our faith lacks an authentic epistemological foundation, a challenge from an all-bad Freud can only be perceived as something to avoid at all costs.

The collapse of one's internal world, to be sure, is an unsettling prospect. For example, many seminarians have experienced the so-called rug being pulled out from under their epistemological framework. Having to deal, for the first time, with such disciplines as the psychology of religion, biblical criticism, world religions, and feminism calls into question a religious faith of the first naïveté. Seminarians, at this point, can either fall back upon certain psychological defenses—for instance, splitting—or they can engage these disciplines that challenge their faith and, in the process, discover that the disciplines are in fact bearers of some aspect of the truth. The reality is that some will see an engagement with various hermeneutics of suspicion as an opportunity, while others will perceive this to be little more than an unmitigated threat to their emotional and spiritual well-being.

In regard to those individuals resistant to a hermeneutics of suspicion, it might do us well to demonstrate sensitivity and understanding, if not empathy, since the collapse of one's epistemological framework, no matter how beneficial in the long run, is never pleasant at the time. In fact, the experience will evoke, in the words of Søren Kierkegaard, *fear* and *trembling*. To those who see the value of holding their faith in tension with a Freudian hermeneutics of suspicion, we can extend our enthusiastic support, while, at the same time, encouraging them to be realistic about the arduousness of the dialectical process. Moreover, we should not be surprised if believers, from time to time, even those in possession of a fully examined faith of the second naïveté, yearn for the time in their lives when they were self-containedly anchored within a religious faith of the first naïveté. In other words, it is safe to assume that a part of the self will always long for that unambiguous time in the past, when it had absolute knowledge and perfect certainty.

The religious believer, then, by firmly holding the truth of Freudian theory in dialectical tension with the truth of religious faith, will be forced to relinquish the innocence and naïveté of the past, and the epistemological certainty that had hitherto precluded any ambiguity. Paradise, it would certainly seem, has been lost forever. That said, believers, if they wish to have a faith credible for today's rather complicated world, have no choice but to begin peeling away the unexamined layers of their faith. Freud and the culture of modernity issued a powerful challenge to the religious community, to the extent that believers must now take the critique to heart in order to formulate an educated and informed response. Moving from one level of religious faith to another, however, especially if the first level has been characterized by unreflection, will surely involve no shortage of emotional and spiritual dissonance. Naturally, the believer, for a period of time, will feel like a fish out of water, particularly the familiar waters of simplicity and certitude. For the first time, the individual must attempt to live with the inherent ambiguities of human living and those associated with religious faith. In terms of the latter, the believer will need to come to terms with the fact that God has a transcendent role as well as a more immanent role in the human psyche.

Having one's internal world turned upside down, even if it does prepare the way for greater psychological and spiritual development, is never pleasant. In fact, it is rather painful. Consequently, believers might be tempted to sidestep a Freudian hermeneutics of suspicion, because of its innate potential to disrupt our inner world. And, while we do not want to minimize the emotional and spiritual pain of a believer whose inner world feels on the verge of collapse, we must nevertheless acknowledge an even greater pain, one that is even more debilitating: the pain of diminishing ego and spiritual strength, which becomes more pronounced every time we feel we do not have the necessary internal resources needed to engage someone like Freud. We are further diminished when our only recourse is to *react* to Freudian theory out of our defenses, most notably, that of splitting off an all-bad Freud from an all-good religious faith.

Whether we decide to engage Freud and his theory of religion or not, the fact is there will be psychical pain either way, in one form or another. On the one hand, the pain that results from a serious engagement with psychoanalysis will be the *pain of growth*, or growing pains, which inevitably will result in a strengthened ego and revitalized religious faith. On the other hand, the pain that results from consistently avoiding any and all hermeneutics of suspicion will be the *pain of diminishment*, resulting in the diminution of ego and faith. It must be remembered that reinforced psychical defenses— for instance, splitting, anger, distancing, indifference, and rationalization— are not indicative of genuine ego strength or a mature religious faith. Rather, it is actually the opposite: strong defenses are an indication of a weakened ego and a fragile belief system. Thus, because of varying degrees of ego strength, it will be important to tailor Freudian theory to a particular believer or group of believers, depending on the person's individual or the group's collective ego strength. Helping those we are working with *prepare* for an engagement with psychoanalysis might be every bit as important as the engagement itself.

In the future, it would be worth exploring, in greater detail, if there really is something akin to splitting at work within the psyche of the believer who adamantly refuses to have anything to do with Freud. Althea Horner, in *Object Relations and the Developing Ego in Therapy*, observes that clients who resort to the defense of splitting create for themselves the illusion of psychical wholeness. These individuals, she points out, look exclusively for "an object of certain attributes who responds in such a manner that the good-self identity is maintained."[3] Horner's "object of certain attributes," as we might expect from an object relations theorist, is the psychical image or representation of a parent, friend, spouse or, transferentially, a therapist or counselor. The object of certain attributes, however, could also be God, or, more accurately, one's psychical image of God. Hypothetically, then, we might say that certain believers maintain a good self-identity by associating exclusively with images of a perfect God and a perfect religious faith, both of which are seemingly devoid of any "contaminative" influences, such as Freudian theory.

Additionally, it would be important to develop more practical strategies for helping believers prepare for, and live more confidently within, the dialectical tension between a hermeneutics of suspicion and a hermeneutics of belief and meaning. These strategies would help believers find a healthy middle ground between religious idealism, where God and faith are seen as completely separate from the realities of human living, and Freudian reductionism, where God and faith become nothing more than derivatives of the human mind. Along the way, believers will become more realistic and accepting of the inherent strengths *and limitations* of their respective faith traditions, as well as the inherent limitations *and strengths* of Freud's interpretation of religion. There will be less need to fall back upon the defensive maneuver of splitting off an all-bad Freud from an all-good religious faith, for the believer will be able to acknowledge that God has both a transcendent and a psychical role.

Epilogue

In chapter 1 I put forward a *description* of the phenomenon under investigation—Freud's theory that religious faith is psychological projection. Then, in chapters 2–4, my focus shifted to a *critical analysis* of the particular phenomenon, by way of the work of Ricoeur, Rizzuto, and Van Herik. Finally, in this last chapter, I have moved the description and critical analysis of Freudian theory to a new level of *constructive interpretation*, by discussing the evocative nature and power of psychoanalysis. What we discovered is that Freud can make us feel anxious and vulnerable, particularly if we are in possession of an unreflective religious faith of the first naïveté. These *primary* feelings, because they are so unsettling, are then converted into secondary feelings or reaction formations, such as outrage or indignation, distancing, indifference, or rationalization. Thus, the two issues that have captured my attention these past few years—Freud's theory that religious faith is the projection of our own subjectivity onto a perceived benevolent Providence and the internal responses Freud and his theory evoke within the psyche of the religious believer—have now been explored in greater detail. My conclusion is that Freud's interpretation of religion and the responses his theory evokes within the believer demand and deserve further investigation.

Future research could and should assume other shapes and forms. For example, future study of Freud's theory of religion as projection, and the responses that theory evokes within the believer, could be theoretical investigations, or they might take the form of an empirical or clinical study. In terms of the former, an empirical researcher could try to determine, statistically, if believers who engage Freud and his theory do in fact have a greater degree of ego and/or spiritual strength than those who keep their distance. Questions to be addressed might include the following: What is the attitude of believers who engage Freud's writings on religion, for a given period of time? How is it similar to, or different from, the attitude of believers who do not engage Freud? Are the designated believers who engage Freud—the experimental group—more satisfied with their religious faith than the believers who do not engage him—the control group? This could also be studied from a clinical perspective, by gathering, much like Rizzuto did, clinical data collected over extended periods of time. Again, questions to be explored might include the following: What, exactly, is occurring in the psyche of the believer, who refuses to even discuss the possibility of God's psychical role? Might this be, anytime an individual images God as exclusively transcendent or entirely "other," something akin to the phenomenon of psychical splitting? Or does the phenomenon need to be called something else?

Another related issue for future consideration has to do with the nature of Freud's impact on Western culture. Since, as Ricoeur claims, the Western world has internalized so much of Freud's theory, and now analyzes itself through this assimilated view, it would be important to determine if Freud was merely *describing* the Western psyche or if he actually, through the application of psychoanalysis, contributed to the *shaping* of it. Or is it both? If his legacy is more than description, then moving beyond Freud may be easier said than done. Finally, it would also be important to know, through further study, if there are believers who can manage to get *around*, rather than *through*, the Freudian interpretation of religion. Is it possible to acquire a postcritical religious faith of the second naïveté, even when we avoid Freud's influential critique? If so, it seems that these particular believers would, at some point, have had to work their way through a comparable hermeneutics of suspicion, one every bit as rigorous as Freud's.

Notes

■ INTRODUCTION ■

1. Van A. Harvey, *Feuerbach and the Interpretation of Religion* (Cambridge: Cambridge University Press, 1995), 25 & 53.

2. In Cornelius Loew, *Myth, Sacred History, and Philosophy* (New York: Harcourt, Brace & World, 1967), 213.

3. David M. Wulff, *Psychology of Religion* (New York: Wiley, 1991), 315.

4. Rodney J. Hunter, gen. ed., *Dictionary of Pastoral Care and Counseling* (Nashville: Abingdon, 1990), 988 & 1003.

5. W. W. Meissner, *Psychoanalysis and Religious Experience* (New Haven: Yale University Press, 1984), 5.

6. Paul Ricoeur, "The Atheism of Freudian Psychoanalysis," *Concilium* 16 (1966): 61.

7. Ana-Maria Rizzuto, *The Birth of the Living God* (Chicago: University of Chicago Press, 1979), x.

8. Judith van Herik, *Freud on Femininity and Faith* (Berkeley: University of California Press, 1982), 1.

9. Sandra M. Schneiders, "A Hermeneutical Approach to the Study of Christian Spirituality," *Christian Spirituality Bulletin* 2 (1994): 13.

10. Schneiders, *The Revelatory Text* (San Francisco: Harper, 1991), 20.

11. Ibid.

12. Schneiders, "Hermeneutical Approach to the Study of Christian Spirituality," 12.

13. James Luther Adams, "Tillich's Interpretation of History," in *The Theology of Paul Tillich*, eds., Charles W. Kegley & Robert W. Bretall (New York: Macmillan, 1961), 297.

■ 1. FREUD'S INTERPRETATION OF RELIGION ■

1. Peter Gay, "Sigmund Freud: A Brief Life," in *Sigmund Freud: An Autobiographical Study* (New York: Norton, 1989), ix.

2. Sigmund Freud, *Civilization and Its Discontents*, vol. 21 of *Standard Edition*, ed. James Strachey (London: Hogarth Press, 1961/1930), 64.

3. Ibid., 65.

4. Freud, *The Ego and the Id*, vol. 19 of *Standard Edition*, ed. Strachey (London: Hogarth Press, 1961/1923), 31.

5. Ibid.

6. Freud, *An Outline of Psycho-Analysis*, vol. 23 of *Standard Edition*, ed. Strachey (London: Hogarth Press, 1964/1940), 189.

7. Freud, *Civilization and Its Discontents*, vol. 21 of *Standard Edition*, 72.

8. Freud, *Outline of Psycho-Analysis*, vol. 23 of *Standard Edition*, 190.

9. Freud, "The Dissolution of the Oedipus Complex," vol. 19 of *Standard Edition*, ed. Strachey (London: Hogarth Press, 1961/1924), 176–177.

10. Freud, *New Introductory Lectures on Psycho-analysis*, vol. 22 of *Standard Edition*, ed. Strachey (London: Hogarth Press, 1964/1933), 73.

11. Freud, *The Future of an Illusion*, vol. 21 of *Standard Edition*, ed. Strachey (London: Hogarth Press, 1961/1927), 11.

12. Strachey, "Editor's Note," in "Mourning and Melancholia," vol. 14 of *Standard Edition*, ed. Strachey (London: Hogarth Press, 1957/1917), 242.

13. Wulff, *Psychology of Religion*, 268.

14. Quote appears in Freud, *Civilization and Its Discontents*, vol. 21 of *Standard Edition*, 134. For the actual context of the quote, see Shakespeare, *Hamlet*, vol. 3 of *The Annotated Shakespeare*, ed. A. L. Rowse (London: Orbis, 1978), 225 (act 3, scene 1).

15. Freud, *Leonardo da Vinci and a Memory of His Childhood*, vol. 11 of *Standard Edition*, ed. Strachey (London: Hogarth Press, 1957/1910), 66. "Pareva che ad ogni ora tremasse, quando si poneva a dipingere, e pero non diede mai fine ad alcuna cosa cominciata, considerando la grandezza dell'arte, tal che egli scorgeva errori in quelle cose, che ad altri parevano miracoli."

16. Note, especially, the following essays: "Some Psychical Consequences of the Anatomical Distinction Between the Sexes," vol. 19 of *Standard Edition*, and "Female Sexuality," vol. 21 of *Standard Edition*.

17. Freud, "The Question of Lay Analysis," vol. 20 of *Standard Edition*, ed. Strachey (London: Hogarth Press, 1959/1926), 212.

18. Carol Gilligan, *In a Different Voice* (Cambridge: Harvard University Press, 1982), 6–7.

19. Freud, "Some Psychical Consequences of the Anatomical Distinction Between the Sexes," vol. 19 of *Standard Edition*, ed. Strachey (London: Hogarth Press, 1961/1925), 254.

20. Freud, *Leonardo da Vinci and a Memory of His Childhood*, vol. 11 of *Standard Edition*, 123.

21. Freud, "Some Psychical Consequences of the Anatomical Distinction Between the Sexes," vol. 19 of *Standard Edition*, 256–257.

22. Ibid., 257.

23. Ibid., 257–258.

24. Freud, "From the History of an Infantile Neurosis," vol. 17 of *Standard Edition*, ed. Strachey (London: Hogarth Press, 1955/1918), 97.

25. Peter Gay, *Freud: A Life for Our Time* (New York: Norton, 1988), footnote on 290.

26. Nancy J. Chodorow, *Feminism and Psychoanalytic Theory* (New Haven: Yale University Press, 1989), 3.

27. Freud, "Some Psychical Consequences of the Anatomical Distinction Between the Sexes," vol. 19 of *Standard Edition*, 258.

28. Obviously, I intend to proceed with this study on Freud, beginning with the final portion of this chapter: how Freud goes about connecting the Oedipus Complex, and specifically, what he calls the "heir of the Oedipus Complex," the superego, to the human individual's need for religion. I would, however, be remiss if I was not candid about my feelings toward Freud, especially the feeling of discomfort I experience when I read his writings on the psychology of women. As I watch my twelve-year-old daughter struggle to grow up in what is still very much—even in the "progressive" San Francisco Bay Area—a man's world, struggle to find her voice in a patriarchal culture that at the very least implicitly nudges her to be content with her socially defined feminine role, I become particularly uncomfortable with talk, coming from Freud or anyone else, of the inherent inferiority of girls and women.

29. Gay, *Freud*, 507.

30. Philip Rieff, *Freud: The Mind of the Moralist* (Garden City, NY: Anchor, 1961), 199–200.

31. Van Herik, "The Feminist Critique of Classical Psychoanalysis," *Concilium* 156 (1982): 84.

32. Rizzuto, *Why Did Freud Reject God?* (New Haven: Yale University Press, 1998), 260.

33. Freud, "The Psychopathology of Everyday Life," vol. 6 of *Standard Edition*, ed. Strachey (London: Hogarth Press, 1960/1901), 19.

34. Ibid., 258–259.

35. Shakespeare, *King Lear*, vol. 3 of *The Annotated Shakespeare*, ed. A. L. Rowse (London: Orbis, 1978), 379.

36. Freud, *Future of an Illusion*, vol. 21 of *Standard Edition*, 24.

37. Ibid., 19.

38. Freud, *Leonardo da Vinci and a Memory of His Childhood*, vol. 11 of *Standard Edition*, 123.

39. Freud, "Obsessive Actions and Religious Practices," vol. 9 of *Standard Edition*, ed. Strachey (London: Hogarth Press, 1959/1907), 117.

40. Ibid. See editor's comment in footnote.

41. Wulff, *Psychology of Religion*, 275.

42. Freud, "Obsessive Actions and Religious Practices," vol. 9 of *Standard Edition*, 124.

43. Ibid., 125.

44. Ibid., 124–125.

45. Ibid., 126–127.

46. Freud, *Totem and Taboo*, vol. 13 of *Standard Edition*, ed. Strachey (London: Hogarth Press, 1955/1913), 1.

47. Michael Palmer, *Freud and Jung on Religion* (London: Routledge, 1997), 22.

48. Freud, *Totem and Taboo*, vol. 13 of *Standard Edition*, 141.

49. Palmer, *Freud and Jung on Religion*, 23.

50. Freud, *Moses and Monotheism: Three Essays*, vol. 23 of *Standard Edition*, ed. Strachey (London: Hogarth Press, 1964/1939), 100.

51. Palmer, *Freud and Jung on Religion*, 30.

52. Freud, *Future of an Illusion*, vol. 21 of *Standard Edition*, 30–31.

53. Herbert Marcuse, *Five Lectures* (Boston: Beacon, 1970), 13.

54. Freud, *Future of an Illusion*, vol. 21 of *Standard Edition*, 38.

55. Freud, *Civilization and Its Discontents*, vol. 21 of *Standard Edition*, 74.

56. Freud, *Ego and the Id*, vol. 19 of *Standard Edition*, 37.

■ 2. WHAT FREUD CAN AND CANNOT TEACH THE RELIGIOUS BELIEVER ■

1. Frederick Crews, ed., *Unauthorized Freud: Doubters Confront a Legend* (New York: Penguin, 1998), xxix.

2. Ibid.

3. Wulff, *Psychology of Religion*, 303.

4. Paul Ricoeur, *Freud and Philosophy*, trans. Denis Savage (New Haven: Yale University Press, 1970), 8.

5. Ibid., 277–278.

6. Ricoeur, *The Philosophy of Paul Ricoeur*, eds. Charles E. Reagan & David Stewart (Boston: Beacon, 1978), 104.

7. Ricoeur, *The Conflict of Interpretations*, ed. Don Ihde (Evanston, IL: Northwestern University Press, 1974), 238.

8. Freud, *Future of an Illusion*, vol. 21 of *Standard Edition*, 24.

9. Charles E. Reagan, *Paul Ricoeur* (Chicago: University of Chicago Press, 1996), 98.

10. Ricoeur, *From Text to Action*, trans. Kathleen Blamey & John B. Thompson (Evanston: Northwestern University Press, 1991), 88.

11. Ricoeur, *Conflict of Interpretations*, 243–244.

12. Donald Capps, *Pastoral Care and Hermeneutics* (Philadelphia: Fortress, 1984), 33.

13. Quoted in Ricoeur, *Conflict of Interpretations*, 243.

14. Ibid., 244.

15. Ricoeur, *Freud and Philosophy*, 458.

16. Hans-Georg Gadamer, *Philosophical Hermeneutics*, ed. & trans. David E. Linge (Berkeley: University of California Press, 1976), 116–117.

17. Freud, *Civilization and Its Discontents*, vol. 21 of *Standard Edition*, 122.

18. Ricoeur, *Conflict of Interpretations*, 195.

19. Don Ihde, "Editor's Introduction," in ibid., xx.

20. Ibid., 131.

21. Ibid., 430.

22. Erik Erikson, *Young Man Luther* (New York: Norton, 1958), 155–156.

23. C. G. Jung, *Answer to Job*, trans. R. F. C. Hull (Princeton: Princeton University, 1958), 74.

24. Ricoeur, *Conflict of Interpretations*, 339.

25. Lewis Rambo, *Understanding Religious Conversion* (New Haven: Yale University Press, 1993), 53.

26. Ricoeur, *Freud and Philosophy*, 545.

27. Ricoeur, *Essays on Biblical Interpretation*, ed. Lewis S. Mudge (Philadelphia: Fortress, 1980) 152.

28. Peter G. Ossorio, "An Overview of Descriptive Psychology," in *The Social Construction of the Person*, eds. Kenneth J. Gergen & Keith E. Davis (New York: Springer-Verlag, 1985), 24.

29. Freud, *Future of an Illusion*, vol. 21 of *Standard Edition*, 24.

30. Ibid., 49.

31. Ricoeur, *Conflict of Interpretations*, 460.

32. Edward E. Sampson, *Ego at the Threshold* (New York: Delta, 1975), 170.

33. Ibid., 159 & 165.

34. Erik Erikson, *Identity and the Life Cycle* (New York: Norton, 1980/1959), 33.

35. Ricoeur, *Conflict of Interpretations*, 472.

36. Ibid., 284–285.

37. Ricoeur, *Freud and Philosophy*, 495.

38. Freud, *Civilization and Its Discontents*, vol. 21 of *Standard Edition*, 145.

39. Ricoeur, *Conflict of Interpretations*, 467.

40. Ibid., 437.

41. Ibid.

42. Freud, *Leonardo da Vinci and a Memory of His Childhood*, vol. 11 of *Standard Edition*, 75–76.

43. Ricoeur, *Freud and Philosophy*, 337.

44. Ricoeur, *Essays on Biblical Interpretation*, 5.

45. Ricoeur, *Freud and Philosophy*, 534.

46. E. S. Fiorenza, "Justified by All Her Children: Struggle, Memory, and Vision," in *The Power of Naming*, ed. Fiorenza (New York: Orbis, 1996), 340.

47. Ricoeur, *Freud and Philosophy*, 151.

48. Ibid., 277.

49. Ricoeur, *Philosophy of Paul Ricoeur*, 222.

50. Ricoeur, *Conflict of Interpretations*, 447.

■ 3. THE PSYCHICAL ROLE OF GOD ■

1. Rizzuto, *Birth of the Living God*, 212. The first quote of Freud is taken from the last paragraph of *The Future of an Illusion*, while the second comes from *Moses and Monotheism*, part 3, section 2, paragraph 6 of the essay, "The Historical Truth."

2. Ibid., 4.

3. C. G. Jung, *Psychology and Religion* (New Haven: Yale University Press, 1938), 73.

4. Martin Buber, *Eclipse of God* (Atlantic Highlands, NJ: Humanities Press International, 1979), 81.

5. Rizzuto, *The Birth of the Living God*, 5.

6. Miriam Greenspan, *A New Approach to Women and Therapy* (Bradenton, FL: Human Services Institute, 1993), 26.

7. Rizzuto, *Birth of the Living God*, 93.

8. Ibid., 94.

9. Ibid., 100.

10. Ibid., 95.

11. Freud, *Civilization and Its Discontents*, vol. 21 of *Standard Edition*, 124.

12. Rizzuto, *Birth of the Living God*, 104.

13. Ibid.

14. Ibid.

15. Freud, *Civilization and Its Discontents*, vol. 21 of *Standard Edition*, 126–127.

16. Freud, *Future of an Illusion*, vol. 21 of *Standard Edition*, 16.

17. Rizzuto, *Birth of the Living God*, 95.

18. Rizzuto, "The Psychological Foundations of Belief in God," in *Toward Moral and Religious Maturity*, ed. C. Brusselmans (Morristown, NJ: Silver Burdett, 1980), p. 132.

19. Freud, *Leonardo da Vinci and a Memory of His Childhood*, vol. 11 of *Standard Edition*, 123.

20. Rizzuto, *Birth of the Living God*, 105.

21. Ibid., 212.

22. D. W. Winnicott, *Playing and Reality* (London: Routledge, 1971), 112–113.

23. Ibid., 114.

24. Rizzuto, *Birth of the Living God*, 109.

25. Ibid.

26. Rizzuto, "Psychological Foundations of Belief in God," 132.

27. Rizzuto, *Birth of the Living God*, 123.

28. Ibid., 127–128.

29. Ibid., 125 & 127–128.

30. Rizzuto, *Why Did Freud Reject God?* (New Haven: Yale University Press, 1998), 169–170.

31. Rizzuto, *Birth of the Living God*, 47.

32. Rizzuto, "Psychological Foundations of Belief in God," 123.

33. Winnicott, *Playing and Reality*, 2.

34. Erik Erikson, *Childhood and Society* (New York: Norton, 1950), 212 & 221.

35. Winnicott, *Playing and Reality*, 100.

36. Rizzuto, "Object Relations and the Formation of the Image of God," *British Journal of Medical Psychology* 47 (1974): 88.

37. Rizzuto, *Birth of the Living God*, 177–178.

38. Ibid., 180.

39. Rizzuto, "Psychological Foundations of Belief in God," 121.

40. Rizzuto, *Why Did Freud Reject God?* 185.

41. Ibid., 268–269.

42. Ibid., 262–263.

■ 4. THE RELATION BETWEEN RELIGIOUS AND GENDER PSYCHOLOGY ■

1. Van Herik, *Freud on Femininity and Faith*, 1.

2. Ibid., 2.

3. Van Herik, "Feminist Critique of Classical Psychoanalysis," 83–86.

4. See Diane Jonte-Pace's recent book, *Speaking the Unspeakable: Religion Misogyny, and the Uncanny Mother in Freud's Cultural Texts* (Berkeley: University of California Press, 2001), for an informative discussion of feminist approaches to Freud. Her description of a *critical* feminist perspective and an *inclusive* feminist perspective corresponds to the two feminist views highlighted by Van Herik. Jonte-Pace includes a third approach, namely, an *analytic* feminist perspective, which may in fact correspond to Van Herik's method.

5. Mary Daly, *Beyond God the Father* (Boston: Beacon, 1973), 149.

6. Van Herik, *Freud on Femininity and Faith*, 194.

7. Ibid., 35.

8. Freud, *Future of an Illusion*, vol. 21 of *Standard Edition*, 30–31.

9. Van Herik, *Freud on Femininity and Faith*, 103.

10. Ibid., 17–18.

11. Ibid., 99.

12. Nancy Chodorow, *The Reproduction of Mothering* (Berkeley: University of California Press, 1978), 176.

13. Van Herik, *Freud on Femininity and Faith*, 103.

14. Freud, "Some Psychical Consequences of the Anatomical Distinction Between the Sexes," vol. 19 of *Standard Edition*, 257.

15. Ricoeur, *Freud and Philosophy*, 327.

16. Van Herik, *Freud on Femininity and Faith*, 101.

17. Ibid., 107–108.

18. Ibid., 111.

19. Ibid., 113.

20. Ibid., 116.

21. Freud, "On Narcissism: An Introduction," vol. 14 of *Standard Edition*, ed. Strachey (London: Hogarth Press, 1957/1914), 88–89.

22. See, for example, "Civilized Sexual Morality and Modern Nervousness," in vol. 9 of *Standard Edition*. Here, Freud highlights the double standard of marriage: men, if they are unhappily married, have various outlets for their repressed sexual energy—the brothel, work, and so forth—while unhappily married women have no such outlets, since they are confined to the home.

23. Van Herik, "Feminist Critique of Classical Psychoanalysis," 85.

24. Freud, "On Narcissism," vol. 14 of *Standard Edition*, 89.

25. Freud, "Three Essays on the Theory of Sexuality," vol. 7 of *Standard Edition*, ed. Strachey (London: Hogarth Press, 1953/1905), 227.

26. Van Herik, *Freud on Femininity and Faith*, 133.

27. Ibid., 134.

28. Freud, *New Introductory Lectures on Psycho-analysis*, vol. 22 of *Standard Edition*, 129.

29. Van Herik, *Freud on Femininity and Faith*, 135.

30. Ibid., 200.

31. Juliet Mitchell, *Psychoanalysis and Feminism* (New York: Vintage, 1974), 403 & 406.

32. Chodorow, *Reproduction of Mothering*, 152.

33. Van Herik, *Freud on Femininity and Faith*, 138.

34. Ibid., 135.

35. Ibid., 108.

36. Ibid., 109.

37. Ibid., 192.

38. Ricoeur, *Freud and Philosophy*, 245.

39. Sander L. Gilman, *Freud, Race, and Gender* (Princeton: Princeton University Press, 1993), 198.

40. Freud, *Moses and Monotheism: Three Essays*, vol. 23 of *Standard Edition*, 118.

41. Van Herik, *Freud on Femininity and Faith*, 143–144.

42. Ibid., 151.

43. Ibid., 144.

44. Ibid.

45. Ibid., 162.

46. Ibid., 166.

47. Ibid., 199.
48. Wulff, *Psychology of Religion*, 312.
49. Van Herik, *Freud on Femininity and Faith*, 194.
50. Ibid., 196.
51. Ibid., 193.

■ 5. BEYOND EITHER-OR:
TOWARD A CONSTRUCTIVE REENGAGEMENT WITH FREUD ■

1. Otto Kernberg, *Borderline Conditions and Pathological Narcissism* (Northvale, NJ: Jason Aronson, 1985), 28.

2. Ibid., 29.

3. Althea Horner, *Object Relations and the Developing Ego in Therapy* (Northvale, NJ: Jason Aronson, 1984), 258.

Bibliography

American Psychiatric Association. 1994. *Diagnostic and Statistical Manual of Mental Disorders.* 4th ed. Washington, DC: Author.

Banks, L. 1973. "Religion as Projection: A Re-appraisal of Freud's Theory." In *Religious Studies* 9: 401–426.

Beit-Hallahmi, Benjamin, & Argyle, Michael. 1997. *The Psychology of Religious Behavior, Belief and Experience.* London: Routledge.

Belenky, Mary Field et al. 1986. *Women's Ways of Knowing: The Development of Self, Voice, and Mind.* New York: Basic.

Berger, Peter. 1965. "Towards a Sociological Understanding of Psychoanalysis." In *Social Research* 32: 26–41.

Berger, Peter. 1967. *The Sacred Canopy.* Garden City, NY: Doubleday.

Becker, Ernst. 1973. *The Denial of Death.* New York: Free Press.

Boisen, Anton. 1936. *The Exploration of the Inner World.* Chicago: Willett, Clark.

Breuer, J., & Freud, S. 1955 (1895). *Studies on Hysteria.* Ed. & trans. J. Strachey. London: Hogarth.

Brown, Norman O. 1959. *Life Against Death: The Psychoanalytic Meaning of History.* Middletown, CN: Wesleyan University.

Browning, Don S. 1991. *A Fundamental Practical Theology: Descriptive and Strategic Proposals.* Minneapolis: Fortress.

Buber, Martin. 1979. *Eclipse of God.* Atlantic Highlands, NJ: Humanities Press International.

Byrnes, Joseph F. 1984. *The Psychology of Religion.* New York: Free Press.

Capps, Donald. 1984. *Pastoral Care and Hermeneutics.* Philadelphia: Fortress.

Chinnici, Rosemary. 1992. *Can Women Re-Image the Church?* New York: Paulist.

Chodorow, Nancy. 1978. *The Reproduction of Mothering.* Berkeley: University of California Press.

Chodorow, Nancy. 1989. *Feminism and Psychoanalytic Theory.* New Haven: Yale University Press.

Corsini, Raymond J., & Wedding, Danny, eds. 1995. *Current Psychotherapies.* Itasca, IL: F. E. Peacock.

Crews, Frederick, ed. 1998. *Unauthorized Freud: Doubters Confront a Legend.* New York: Penguin.

DeMarinis, Valerie. 1993. *Critical Caring.* Louisville: Westminster/John Knox.

DiCenso, James J. 1999. *The Other Freud: Religion, Culture, and Psychoanalysis.* London: Routledge.

Eichenbaum, Luise, & Orbach, Susie. 1983. *Understanding Women.* New York: Basic.

Ellenberger, Henri. 1970. *The Discovery of the Unconscious.* New York: Basic.

Erikson, Erik. 1950. *Childhood and Society.* New York: Norton.

Erikson, Erik. 1958. *Young Man Luther.* New York: Norton.

Erikson, Erik. 1980 (1959). *Identity and the Life Cycle.* New York: Norton.

Feuerbach, Ludwig. 1957 (1841). *The Essence of Christianity.* Trans. G. Eliot. New York: Harper.

Fiorenza, E. S., ed. 1996. *The Power of Naming.* New York: Orbis.

Flax, Jane. 1990. *Thinking Fragments: Psychoanalysis, Feminism, and Postmodernism in the Contemporary West.* Berkeley: University of California Press.

Freud, S. 1900. *The Interpretation of Dreams.* In *Standard Edition,* Vols. 4 & 5.

Freud, S. 1901. *The Psychopathology of Everyday Life.* In *Standard Edition,* Vol. 6.

Freud, S. 1905. *Three Essays on the Theory of Sexuality.* In *Standard Edition,* Vol. 7.

Freud, S. 1907. "Obsessive Actions and Religious Practices." In *Standard Edition,* Vol. 9.

Freud, S. 1908a. "Character and Anal Erotism." In *Standard Edition,* Vol. 9.

Freud, S. 1908b. "Civilized Sexual Morality and Modern Nervousness." In *Standard Edition,* Vol. 9.

Freud, S. 1910. *Leonardo da Vinci and a Memory of His Childhood.* In *Standard Edition,* Vol. 11.

Freud, S. 1911. "Psycho-Analytic Notes on an Autobiographical Account of a Case of Paranoia (Dementia Paranoides)." In *Standard Edition,* Vol. 12.

Freud, S. 1913. *Totem and Taboo: Some Points of Agreement Between the Mental Lives of Savages and Neurotics.* In *Standard Edition,* Vol. 13.

Freud, S. 1914a. "The Moses of Michelangelo." In *Standard Edition,* Vol. 13.

Freud, S. 1914b. "On Narcissism: An Introduction." In *Standard Edition,* Vol. 14.

Freud, S. 1915. "Thoughts for the Times on War and Death." In *Standard Edition,* Vol. 14.

Freud, S. 1916–1917. *Introductory Lectures on Psycho-Analysis.* In *Standard Edition,* Vols. 15 & 16.

Freud, S. 1917. "Mourning and Melancholia." In *Standard Edition,* Vol. 14.

Freud, S. 1918. "From the History of an Infantile Neurosis." In *Standard Edition,* Vol. 17.

Freud, S. 1920. *Beyond the Pleasure Principle.* In *Standard Edition,* Vol. 18.

Freud, S. 1921. *Group Psychology and the Analysis of the Ego.* In *Standard Edition,* Vol. 18.

Freud, S. 1923a. *The Ego and the Id.* In *Standard Edition,* Vol. 19.

Freud, S. 1923b. "A Seventeenth-Century Demonological Neurosis." In *Standard Edition*, Vol. 19.

Freud, S. 1924. "The Dissolution of the Oedipus Complex." In *Standard Edition*, Vol. 19.

Freud, S. 1925a. *An Autobiographical Study*. In *Standard Edition*, Vol. 20.

Freud, S. 1925b. "Some Psychical Consequences of the Anatomical Distinction Between the Sexes." In *Standard Edition*, Vol. 19.

Freud, S. 1926a. "Address to the Society of B'nai B'rith." In *Standard Edition*, Vol. 20.

Freud, S. 1926b. *The Question of Lay Analysis: Conversations with an Impartial Person*. In *Standard Edition*, Vol. 20.

Freud, S. 1927. *The Future of an Illusion*. In *Standard Edition*, Vol. 21.

Freud, S. 1928. "A Religious Experience." In *Standard Edition*, Vol. 21.

Freud, S. 1930. *Civilization and Its Discontents*. In *Standard Edition*, Vol. 21.

Freud, S. 1931. "Female Sexuality." In *Standard Edition*, Vol. 21.

Freud, S. 1933. *New Introductory Lectures on Psycho-Analysis*. In *Standard Edition*, Vol. 22.

Freud, S. 1939. *Moses and Monotheism: Three Essays*. In *Standard Edition*, Vol. 23.

Freud, S. 1940. *An Outline of Psycho-Analysis*. In *Standard Edition*, Vol. 23.

Freud, S. 1953–1974. *The Standard Edition of the Complete Psychological Works of Freud* (24 vols.). Trans. under the general editorship of J. Strachey. London: Hogarth & Institute of Psycho-Analysis.

Freud, S. 1960. *Letters of Sigmund Freud*. Ed. E. L. Freud & trans. T. & J. Stern. New York: Basic.

Freud, S. 1985. *The Complete Letters of Sigmund Freud to Wilhelm Fliess, 1887–1904*. Ed. & trans. J. M. Masson. Cambridge: Belknap/Harvard University.

Gadamer, Hans-Georg. 1976. *Philosophical Hermeneutics*. Berkeley: University of California Press.

Gadamer, Hans-Georg. 1988. *Truth and Method*. New York: Crossroad.

Gay, Peter. 1987. *A Godless Jew: Freud, Atheism, and the Making of Psychoanalysis*. New Haven: Yale University Press.

Gay, Peter. 1988. *Freud: A Life for Our Time*. New York: Norton.

Gay, Volney. 1979. *Freud on Ritual: Reconstruction and Critique*. Missoula, MT: Scholars Press.

Gergen, Kenneth J., & Davis, Keith E., eds. 1985. *The Social Construction of the Person*. New York: Springer-Verlag.

Gerkin, Charles V. 1984. *The Living Human Document*. Nashville: Abingdon.

Gilligan, Carol. 1982. *In a Different Voice: Psychological Theory and Women's Development*. Cambridge: Harvard University Press.

Gilman, Sander L. 1993. *Freud, Race, and Gender*. Princeton: Princeton University Press.

Greenspan, Miriam. 1983. *A New Approach to Women and Therapy*. Bradenton, FL: Human Services Institute.

Hall, C. S., & Lindzey, G. 1970. *Theories of Personality*. New York: Wiley.

Harvey, Van A. 1995. *Feuerbach and the Interpretation of Religion*. Cambridge: Cambridge University.

Homans, Peter. 1970. *Theology after Freud*. Indianapolis: Bobbs-Merrill.

Homans, Peter. 1979. *Jung in Context: Modernity and the Making of a Psychology*. Chicago: University of Chicago Press.

Homans, Peter. 1989. *The Ability to Mourn: Disillusionment and the Social Origins of Psychoanalysis*. Chicago: University of Chicago Press.

Horner, Althea. 1984. *Object Relations and the Developing Ego in Therapy*. Northvale, NJ: Jason Aronson.

Horney, Karen. 1967. *Feminine Psychology*. Ed. H. Kelman. London: Routledge & Kegan Paul.

Howard, Roy J. 1982. *Three Faces of Hermeneutics*. Berkeley: University of California Press.

Hunter, Rodney J., gen. ed. 1990. *Dictionary of Pastoral Care and Counseling*. Nashville: Abingdon.

Jacobs, Janet, & Capps, Donald, eds. 1997. *Religion, Society and Psychoanalysis: Readings in Contemporary Theory*. Boulder, CO: Westview.

Jones, Ernest. 1953–1957. *The Life and Work of Sigmund Freud* (3 vols.). New York: Basic.

Jonte-Pace, Diane. 1987. "Object Relations Theory, Mothering, and Religion: Toward a Feminist Psychology of Religion." In *Horizons* 14: 310–327.

Jonte-Pace, Diane. 2001. *Speaking the Unspeakable: Religion, Misogyny, and the Uncanny Mother in Freud's Cultural Texts*. Berkeley: University of California Press.

Jonte-Pace, Diane, & Parsons, William, eds. 2000. *Psychology and Religion: Mapping the Terrain*. London: Routledge.

Jung, C. G. 1938. *Psychology and Religion*. New Haven: Yale University Press.

Jung, C. G. 1958. *Answer to Job*. Trans. R. F. C. Hull. Princeton: Princeton University.

Kernberg, Otto. 1979. *Borderline Conditions and Pathological Narcissism*. Northvale, NJ: Jason Aronson.

Kernberg, Otto. 1984. *Object Relations Theory and Clinical Psychoanalysis*. Northvale, NJ: Jason Aronson.

Kung, Hans. 1979. *Freud and the Problem of God*. New Haven: Yale University Press.

Lear, Jonathan. 1990. *Love and Its Place in Nature: A Philosophical Interpretation of Freudian Psychoanalysis*. New York: Farrar.

Loew, Cornelius. 1967. *Myth, Sacred History, and Philosophy*. New York: Harcourt, Brace, & World.

Marcuse, Herbert. 1962. *Eros and Civilization: A Philosophical Inquiry into Freud*. Boston: Beacon.

Marcuse, Herbert. 1970. "Freedom and Freud's Theory of Instincts." In *Five Lectures: Psychoanalysis, Politics, and Utopia*. Trans. J. J. Shapiro & S. M. Weber. Boston: Beacon. Pp. 1–43.

McDargh, John. 1983. *Psychoanalytic Object Relations Theory and the Study of Religion.* New York: University Press of America.

Meissner, William W. 1984. *Psychoanalysis and Religious Experience.* New Haven: Yale University Press.

Miller, Jean Baker. 1986. *Toward a New Psychology of Women.* Boston: Beacon.

Mitchell, Juliet. 1974. "On Freud and the Distinction Between the Sexes." In *Women and Analysis: Dialogues on Psychoanalytic Views of Femininity.* Ed. J. Strouse. New York: Viking. Pp. 27–36.

Mitchell, Juliet. 1974. *Psychoanalysis and Feminism.* New York: Random.

Palmer, Michael. 1997. *Freud and Jung on Religion.* London: Routledge.

Palmer, Richard E. 1969. *Hermeneutics.* Evanston, IL: Northwestern University Press.

Rambo, Lewis. 1993. *Understanding Religious Conversion.* New Haven: Yale University Press.

Ricoeur, Paul. 1960. *The Symbolism of Evil.* Trans. E. Buchanan. New York: Harper.

Ricoeur, Paul. 1966. "The Atheism of Freudian Psychoanalysis." In *Concilium* 16: 59–72.

Ricoeur, Paul. 1970. *Freud and Philosophy.* New Haven: Yale University Press.

Ricoeur, Paul. 1974. *The Conflict of Interpretations.* Ed. Don Ihde. Evanston, IL: Northwestern University Press.

Ricoeur, Paul. 1978. *The Philosophy of Paul Ricoeur.* Eds. Charles E. Reagan & David Stewart. Boston: Beacon.

Ricoeur, Paul. 1980. *Essays on Biblical Interpretation.* Ed. Lewis S. Mudge. Philadelphia: Fortress.

Rieff, Philip. 1959. *Freud: The Mind of the Moralist.* Garden City, NY: Doubleday.

Rieff, Philip. 1966. *The Triumph of the Therapeutic: Uses of Faith after Freud.* New York: Harper.

Rizzuto, Ana-Maria. 1974. "Object Relations and the Formation of the Image of God." In *British Journal of Medical Psychology* 47: 83–99.

Rizzuto, Ana-Maria. 1976. "Freud, God, the Devil and the Theory of Object Representation." In *International Review of Psycho-Analysis* 31: 165.

Rizzuto, Ana-Maria. 1979. *The Birth of the Living God: A Psychoanalytic Study.* Chicago: University of Chicago Press.

Rizzuto, Ana-Maria. 1980. "The Psychological Foundations of Belief in God." In *Toward Moral and Religious Maturity.* Ed. C. Brusselmans. Morristown, NJ: Silver Burdett Co. Pp. 115–135.

Rizzuto, Ana-Maria. 1998. *Why Did Freud Reject God?* New Haven: Yale University Press.

Russell, Letty. 1993. *Church in the Round: Feminist Interpretation of the Church.* Louisville: Westminster/John Knox.

Sampson, Edward E. 1975. *Ego at the Threshold.* New York: Delta.

Sampson, Edward E. 1993. *Celebrating the Other.* Boulder, CO: Westview.

Schneiders, Sandra M. 1991. *The Revelatory Text.* San Francisco: Harper.

Schneiders, Sandra M. 1994. "A Hermeneutical Approach to the Study of Christian Spirituality." In *Christian Spirituality Bulletin* 2: 9–14.

Smith Jr., Archie. 1982. *The Relational Self*. Nashville: Abingdon.

Smith, Joseph, & Handelman, Susan, eds. 1990. *Psychoanalysis and Religion*. Baltimore: Johns Hopkins University Press.

Stein, E. V. 1968. *Guilt: Theory and Therapy*. Philadelphia: Westminster.

Stein, E. V. 1983. "Freud and the Christian Faith." In *Pacific Theological Review* 16: 19–26.

Stein, E. V. 1984. "The Psychological Roots of Self and Faith." In *Pacific Theological Review* 18: 41–51.

Stokes, Allison. 1985. *Ministry after Freud*. New York: Pilgrim.

Sulloway, Frank. 1979. *Freud, Biologist of the Mind: Beyond the Psychoanalytic Legend*. New York: Basic.

Van Herik, Judith. 1982. *Freud on Femininity and Faith*. Berkeley: University of California Press.

Van Herik, Judith. 1982. "The Feminist Critique of Classical Psychoanalysis." In *Concilium* 156: 83–86.

Winnicott, D. W. 1966. *The Maturational Process and the Facilitating Environment*. New York: International University Press.

Winnicott, D. W. 1971. *Playing and Reality*. New York: Basic.

Wulff, David M. 1991. *Psychology of Religion*. New York: Wiley.

Index

Printed in the United States
64467LVS00002B/31-57

9 780791 456545